OCR HISTORY B

AS

Historical Explanation and Using Historical Evidence

Angela Anderson and Andrew Pickering with Keith Lockton and Allan Todd | Series editor: Martin D W Jones

www.heinemann.co.uk

✓ Free online support
✓ Useful weblinks
✓ 24 hour online ordering

01865 888080

OCR
RECOGNISING ACHIEVEMENT

Heinemann

Official Publisher Partnership

Heinemann is an imprint of Pearson Education Limited, a company Incorporated in England and Wales, having its registered office at Edinburgh Gate, Harlow, Essex, CM20 2JE. Registered company number: 872828. www.heinemann.co.uk. Heinemann is a registered trademark of Pearson Education Limited

Text © Angela Anderson and Andrew Pickering 2008

First published 2008

12 11 10 09 08

10 9 8 7 6 5 4 3 2 1

British Library Cataloguing in Publication Data is available from the British Library on request.

ISBN 978-0435312350

Edited by Susan Ross

Original illustrations © Pearson Education Limited.

Cover photo ©Corbis

Picture research by Zooid

Typeset by Dickidot

Printed in UK by Scotprint Ltd

The author and publisher would like to thank the following individuals and organisations for permission to reproduce photographs and copyright material:

Pp56 Hereford Cathedral, Herefordshire, UK/Bridgeman Art Library; Pp58 Hulton Archive/Getty Images; Pp60 David King Collection; Pp61 Mary Evans Picture Library/Mary Evans Picture Library; Pp68 INTERFOTO/Mary Evans Picture Library; Pp 71 akg-images; Pp74 Galleria dell' Accademia, Florence, Italy/Bridgeman Art Library; Pp78 Church of St.Leonard, St.Leonards, Herefordshire, UK/Bridgeman Art Library; Pp 82 Manchester Art Gallery, UK/Bridgeman Art Library; Pp87 Mary Evans Picture Library; Pp93 Steve Schapiro/Corbis UK Ltd.

Pp 3,5 Extract from The Wars of the Roses and the Yorkist Kings by J Warren, Hodder & Stoughton, 1995,by permission of Hodder & Stoughton Ltd; Pp 15/16 Extract from The French Revolution by L Kekewich amd S Rose, Longman 1990, ISBN 0-582 06281 0, reproduced by permission of Pearson Education; Pp33 Extract from The European Reformation by A Armstrong, Heinemann, 2002, by permission of Harcourt Education; Pp34-36 Extracts from Lenin and the Russian Revolution by S Philips, Heinemann 2000, by permission of Harcourt Education; Pp66 Extract from If the Nazis had Come by Comer Clarke, Consul Books, 1962; Pp00 Extract from Reading Historical Documents by J Fines, Basil Blackwell, 1988, by permission of Wiley-Blackwell Publishing; Pp71 Extracts from Blood of the Vikings by Julian Richards, Hodder & Stoughton 2001, by permission of Hodder& Stoughton; Pp75 Extract from Lost Villages by Linda Viner, Dovecote Press, 2002, by permission of Dovecote Press; Pp84 Extract from Democracy and Reform:1815-1885 by D G Wright, Longman 1970, reproduced by permission of Pearson Education; 89 Extract from Years of Nationalism: European History, 1815-90 by L W Cowie and R Wolfson, by permission of Hodder & Stoughton Ltd;

Every effort has been made to contact copyright holders of material reproduced in this book. Any omissions will be rectified in subsequent printings if notice is given to the publishers.

Websites

There are links to relevant websites in this book. In order to ensure that the links are up-to-date, that the links work, and that the sites are not inadvertently linked to sites that could be considered offensive, we have made the links available on the Heinemann website at www.heinemann.co.uk/hotlinks. When you access the site, the express code is 350P

Contents

This book, *Historical Explanation and Using Historical Evidence*, is designed to support OCR's History B specification. It is divided into two parts: Historical Explanation (Units F981/F982) and Using Historical Evidence (Units F983/F984). Each part is divided into two chapters. The first part outlines the theory and the second demonstrates use of that theory through a series of case studies based on the AS topics in the specification. Each part also has detailed exam preparation and support in the Exam Café, with further support materials on the CD-ROM.

How to use this book

Engagement with historical thinking needs to run throughout teaching and learning for OCR History B. *Historical Explanation and Using Historical Evidence* has been written specifically to provide teachers and students with a taught course on the methodological understanding required for every topic and in every exam unit.

Each unit in OCR GCE History B is designed to be introduced through a consideration of the historical concepts. The modes of historical thinking should preface the start of every new topic, and might also make valuable conclusions too. Teaching programmes might adopt a dynamic pattern of alternating between theory and topic content, the one buttressing, developing and reinforcing the other. This book will allow you to adopt either approach.

Methods of assessment

The AS GCE is made up of two units that are externally assessed. There are four units at AS of which candidates do two, either:

- Historical Explanation – British History, with Using Historical Evidence – Non-British History

- Historical Explanation – Non-British History, with Using Historical Evidence – British History.

Historical Explanation is assessed by a written paper, 1.5 hours for 50 marks. Candidates answer **one** question from a choice of two questions for their chosen period. Questions are structured in two parts; two out of the three historical explanations (explaining events, explaining ideas, attitudes and beliefs, explaining actions) will be examined in each two-part question.

Using Historical Evidence is assessed by a written paper, 1.5 hours for 50 marks. Candidates answer **two** questions for their chosen period. The first question is worth a maximum of 35 marks, the second question a maximum of 15 marks. Questions are source based with five to seven sources per option. The first question requires students to use the sources and their own knowledge to evaluate and possibly amend an interpretation. The second question will require candidates to analyse the sources for their usefulness and their problems.

How to use this book

This book has been specifically written to support you through the OCR B GCE History course. **Historical Explanation and Using Historical Evidence** will help you to understand the theory and concepts that underlie the topics you are studying. It can be used as a reference throughout your course as well as an introduction to the theory element of the specification.

You should also refer back to this book during your revision. The Exam Café sections and on the CD-ROM will be particularly helpful as you prepare for your exam.

The book includes the following features:

Sources A wide variety of sources throughout the book will allow you to practise your historical skills.

Activities These have been designed to help you understand the specification content and develop your historical skills.

Think like an historian You should be thinking like an historian throughout your history course. Questions are asked about the content to encourage you to think like this; sometimes you really should just think through these ideas!

Case study 1: The Partition of Ireland

In Chapter 1, we established a brief causal explanation of why Ireland was partitioned

Case studies These illustrate the historical theory in context and are taken from the eight topic options. Most of the examples can be applied in some way to the topic you are studying for your AS exam.

Exam tips These highlight common errors and give you advice about exam preparation to help you achieve the best grade you can.

Definitions Definitions of new words can be found in the margin close to where the word appears in the text to help put the word in context.

Quick facts Additional background information in the margin will give you the wider context on a topic.

Margin questions These will encourage you to apply historical enquiry techniques to topics and sources.

Exam Café In our unique Exam Café you'll find lots of ideas to help you prepare for your exams. You'll see the Exam Café at the end of each unit. You can **Relax** because there's handy revision advice from fellow students, **Refresh your memory** with summaries and checklists of the key ideas you need to revise and **Get that result!** through practising exam-style questions, accompanied by hints and tips on getting the very best grades.

Free CD-ROM

You'll also find a free CD-ROM in the back of this book. On the CD you will find an electronic version of the student book, powered by LiveText. As well as the student book and LiveText tools, you will also find an interactive Exam Café. This contains a wealth of interactive exam preparation material: interactive multiple-choice questions, revision flashcards, exam-style questions with student answers and examiner feedback and much more!

Series Editor introduction

Congratulations! You are studying the most exciting and useful of the six AS/A2 History specifications. OCR's History B gets to grips with what History actually is. Famously, the author of *The Go-Between*, L.P. Hartley said, 'The past is a foreign country; they do things differently there.' Spec B will teach you how to understand that other world. It explains:

■ how to judge the surviving evidence

■ whow to make sense of the past by putting that evidence together

■ how and why that evidence leads to rival interpretations of the past, and how to measure the significance of people and their actions.

Through spec B, you will see why History is alive with argument and debate, always being rethought and revised. Along the way, you will also learn to assess the motives of the peoples of the past and the consequences of their actions. That matters, for their decisions shaped our world; their tomorrows are our yesterdays.

Heinemann's series of books and CD-ROMs are tailored to meet the requirements of spec B. Whichever topics you are studying, you have to learn how to think like a historian. *Historical Explanation and Using Historical Evidence (AS)* and *Historical Significance and Historical Controversies* (A2) will teach you the skills that you need for success. These books cover all the issues underpinning the eight AS topics of Units F981/F982 Historical Explanation and the eight topics of Units F983/F984 Using Historical Evidence; and the eight A2 topics in Units F985/F986 Historical Controversies and your personal study (Unit F987).

Using this book will develop your thinking and understanding. Ideas and issues are highlighted throughout. Case studies with sources and activities set you problems to consider. 'Think like an historian' encourages you to see the bigger picture. Exam tips work on your question skills. All will help you when you are starting to study a topic as well keeping you on course during the term – and remember to refer back to them when revising for mocks and then the real thing.

Don't overlook the Exam Café sections, which are not just for revision – their focused advice and help are always on hand. The tips, revision checklists and advice show you how to write better essays. 'Get the result!' offers student answers with feedback and advice which should help you to improve your own answers. And the Exam Café CD-ROM has even more to offer!

Understanding historical enquiry

History is not the story of everything that happened. The past is not a one-way street: events might have turned out differently. Equally, the surviving evidence can generate alternative accounts of the past. History starts when comparisons and connections are made. History really comes to life when those comparisons and connections are analysed and their relative importance is established. So, focus on understanding the patterns. The past has to be given meaning.

Be alert to what the sources can offer you. The first step is to mine them for information, but that is using them at the most basic level. The next step is to use them for reference: to illustrate a point or start a discussion. But even at this point, you are still hardly using the sources. You will also need to evaluate them, both singly and as a set. You will need to interpret what is in them. The most effective approach is to use sources as an evidence bank from which to build argument and counter-argument. So interrogate sources carefully. Be forensic and sceptical when you examine, verify and compare evidence – but always treat evidence with respect. Evidence is partial in both senses of the word, that is, incomplete and one-sided. The obvious temptation is to reject such evidence. You may have done that at GCSE, dismissing a source as biased, but look again. If it is one-sided, its very subjectivity is of great value because of the attitudes and prejudices it reveals. Considering such sources will help you 'get under the skin' of the past.

Evidence allows you to infer what was going on, and construct historical accounts. Those accounts will not be copies of the past, but estimations of the past. From those accounts, historians then develop claims (hypotheses) about the past. These are provisional and will be tested by further research. In time, hypotheses are accepted with modifications or rejected and abandoned.

What should historians concentrate on? Explanation and evidence make historical enquiry possible, but the past is not a box of scrabble letters to write anything we please. Feminist history has changed the way that History is researched and written. In the process, it has changed our understanding of the past. Forty years ago, that role was held by economic history, but fashions change. Such things affect the key questions that historians ask and the directions new research takes. The practice of History is dynamic. Historians are always in dialogue with the historical record. 'The facts speak only when the historian calls on them; it is [he or she] who decides which facts to give the floor, and in what order or context' (E. H. Carr (1961) *What is History?* Penguin, p. 11).

Martin D. W. Jones

1 The nature of historical explanation

The historian's job

History is the study of what happened in the past – or is it? The past is a source of human experience, mythology and drama, and many writers, artists, politicians and journalists use it to inform, to entertain and to justify their ideas and beliefs. Shakespeare wrote 'History' plays about medieval kings using language, characters and ideas that belonged to his own time. The plays created an image of those kings and their actions that has long influenced popular perceptions of the past, because the elements of drama and fiction are mixed in with what is considered 'fact', that is, key events that are widely recorded and 'known'. It can be argued that the job of an historian is to distinguish between fact and fiction – and that History is the study of 'what *really* happened' in the past. The question is, how (and how far) can that be done?

THINK LIKE AN HISTORIAN

It has been said that there are no facts in history – only fragments of what people at the time saw, thought and believed. While this is true in some ways, there are events that were so widely seen and recorded by many different people that we can be sure, at least, that the event took place. No one seriously doubts that King Charles I was beheaded at Whitehall on 30 January 1649 – what is still a matter of debate is why.

The 'facts' of history are like bricks – solid blocks of material that can be laid out in different forms and patterns to re-create aspects of the past. They are generally accepted and not the subject of debate. Historians arrange the facts in sequence to tell a story or narrative, and highlight particular facts to describe a situation. Both of these tasks involve a level of skill in selecting facts that are relevant, accurate and capable of creating a coherent picture of the past. Both are important in conveying knowledge to those who study the past, but neither narrative nor description offers what historians are seeking – an *understanding* of what happened that enables them to explain it. The role of explanation in history, and the historian's job, is to link 'facts' in order to explain not only what happened but also why, how and with what effects. Briefly, the role of historical explanation is to turn knowledge into understanding

Turning knowledge into understanding

This is done by asking questions and investigating what happened to find answers. 'What happened' can be analysed using a range of recognised questions such as *why* and *how*, and a number of concepts such as the *nature, significance and impact* of events and situations, in order to explore their meaning more fully, using knowledge of the wider situation. Figure 1.1 sets out this process.

Historians then put together ideas and conclusions and support them by reference to 'the facts' to offer an explanation of the past. You will need to understand two important points about this process:

■ It is based on asking questions about what happened.

■ The answers the historian obtains will depend on both the type of questions asked and their interpretation of the 'facts'.

Therefore, historical explanations have to go beyond the facts to include judgements about what happened, and for this reason, they are not always generally accepted.

Other historians researching the same area may have formed different judgements and therefore historical explanations are suggestions – we call them **hypotheses** – and they are the subject of debate.

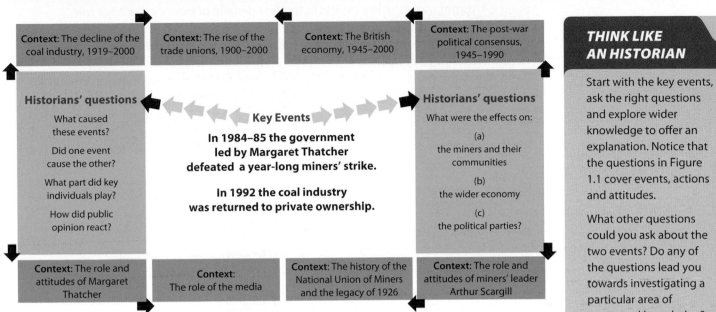

■ Figure 1.1

Using contextual knowledge of the wider situation to turn knowledge into understanding

This process can be illustrated using the two extracts below, which are taken from a text book written for A Level students about the Wars of the Roses and the Yorkist kings. Source 1 is a narrative about the early part of the reign of Henry VI, up to Cade's Revolt in 1450; source 2 describes the role of the king in fifteenth – century England.

Source 1

In 1422, Henry of Windsor, a nine-month-old baby, became King of England as Henry VI. His warrior father, Henry V, had succumbed to dysentery – as deadly to the medieval soldier as a crossbow bolt. In 1431, Henry VI was crowned King of France as well. His English lands and his crown were well served by the royal council that governed in his name, and, when he took full control of his kingdom by 1437, the monarch's powers were undiminished and his inheritance more or less intact. By 1450, virtually everything possible had gone wrong. The king had shown little interest in war. Disastrous failures in the field led to the loss of Normandy to the French in 1450.… At home the king apparently deluged the court factions that he favoured with crown offices and lands. He allowed the Earl of Suffolk (made a duke in 1448) to dominate the Royal Household, and stood by him when he was accused by the Commons of treason over the disasters in France…. The Commons also attempted to get the king to claw back all the grants – of crown lands and the like – which he had scattered among his favourites and so weakened the crown itself. An Act of Resumption – humiliating to the king – was duly passed in 1450, and was followed later in the month by the so-called Cade rebellion. The rebels … wanted punishment for the alleged misdeeds of various royal servants in Kent, where many of them came from; they wanted fairer justice; they wanted the destruction of the remains of the Suffolk faction; and they wanted Henry to rely upon the advice of other great lords whose voices were rarely heard at the king's council. In particular, they singled out Richard, Duke of York, who was of royal blood and seen by some as the childless Henry's heir. Cade's rebellion eventually collapsed: but not before the king had demonstrated a weakness bordering on cowardice in fleeing from his capital.

Adapted from J. Warren (1995)
The Wars of the Roses and the Yorkist Kings
(Access to History), Hodder & Stoughton.

THINK LIKE AN HISTORIAN

Before you read on, consider what questions you could ask to develop a better understanding of the events described in source 1?

Developing understanding

Source 1 summarises the key events in the first decade of Henry's personal rule, culminating in rebellion. Events have been selected and placed in chronological order to create a narrative, but the source does not explain why the rebellion took place or why it should have happened at that time. So far, we have *knowledge* of what happened but not *understanding* of what was going on. If we now question the events to consider their implications, we can begin to develop some ideas.

- The king showed little interest in war and was responsible for military failure. How would people feel about that?

- He apparently favoured one faction of the nobility and rewarded them greatly, to the point of 'weakening the crown'. How?

- This was resented by the 'Commons' – who were they?

- Why did they act against the king's wishes? The grievances outlined in Cade's Revolt suggest some reasons – the dominance of one faction was unpopular, government was unjust and perhaps corrupt, and other great lords wanted a greater role. Did these contribute to the rebellion in some way?

Full answers to these questions would need further research, but already we can suggest some *causes* of the rebellion:

- The king's perceived weakness created a lack of respect.

- He ignored and undervalued powerful men in favour of a small faction.

- Government was seen to be failing both at home and abroad.

What kind of 'facts'?

So far we have questioned the facts – a number of different events and the actions taken by the monarch – and put forward three possible causes to explain the revolt. To go further, we need more information, and perhaps information of a different kind.

Source ② The role of the English king

The king stood outside the three estates of the Church, the nobility and the Commons. He was the head directing the body or, to use another metaphor, the linchpin that held together English society. In the fifteenth century it was believed that the king was placed – as was each member of the three estates – in his position by God. In the king's case this belief was vividly represented through the symbols of the coronation rituals. The king was anointed with holy oil as a sign of God's grace…. The oil was left on the king's head and body for eight days and was then washed off. A little tepid white wine, it seems, cleaned it all away nicely. On occasions the effect of the oil was more than symbolic – the story goes that Henry IV acquired a bumper crop of lice on the royal head.

Although the king could not claim the priestly powers of saying Mass or offering forgiveness for Sins the coronation. ceremonies raised him above ordinary men. To seek to overthrow an anointed king was a sin against God. This did not mean that rebellion never happened, but that it generally did not take the form of an open attempt to depose the king. Incompetence on the part of a king was no excuse for deposition. He inherited a throne by virtue of royal blood, not through passing an interview panel. Does this mean that he had absolute power, that he could rule without needing to consider the wishes of those he governed? The short answer is 'no'. The king could not make, scrap or rule without laws. For laws and taxes he was obliged to get the agreement of a parliament…. War was the king's to decide and declare. His subjects were expected to give him the necessary military

Source 2 The role of the English king (continued)

support in defence of his interests at home and abroad. His interests, note, not theirs. The kingdom was, in theory, the king's personal property, to do with as he wished. But in practice, of course, the actions of a king affected too many people for him to be totally irresponsible or utterly heedless of the interests of others in war and diplomacy. The king was indeed seen as God's appointee, but he was appointed for a purpose: the defence of the realm and his people.

Adapted from J. Warren (1995) *The Wars of the Roses and the Yorkist Kings* (Access to History), Hodder & Stoughton.

Source 2 is primarily a description of a situation – the part played by kings in fifteenth-century English government. Although there is some consideration of the extent of his powers, it does not go far in explaining the implications of the 'facts' used in the description. However, it does poise the question, and the selection of material does make implicit links (that is, links that are implied or suggested rather than put into words) to the king's role and functions that can be explored further. It also differs from source 1 in that it is not focused on events or actions, but on *ideas* – beliefs and attitudes – that influenced what people did, what they expected, and therefore how they were likely to react in different situations. It therefore allows us to view our earlier conclusions about why Henry VI faced a rebellion in a slightly different way, and to ask some different questions about what was going on.

To explore source 2 further, we could ask: If this was the king's role, what qualities would a good king need? We could then use our suggestions to look again at the actions of Henry VI, and consider how far he met the requirements for an effective king and why his actions might have created discontent. Would this review add to or reinforce our suggested causes of Cade's Revolt? Source 2 could also raise new questions. If the king was God's anointed, why did Cade's followers rebel against him? What was the nature of the rebellion, and what did the rebels hope to achieve? By using the two sources together, we can explore the causes of the revolt, the motives of the rebels and the reasons for its collapse more fully, and so start to offer an *explanation* of what happened.

Cade's Revolt was an *event*, but it can also be seen as an *action* taken by the rebels. To explain an event, we have to look at causes; to explain actions, we tend to look at motives and intentions – what the rebels hoped to achieve – and the ideas or attitudes that influenced them.

THINK LIKE AN HISTORIAN

How would these ideas and attitudes affect the way people saw the king – what they expected of him, and how they would react to what he did?

ACTIVITY

To illustrate the difference, use sources 1 and 2 to answer the following questions:

1. Why was Henry VI facing rebellion by 1450?

2. Why did men take up arms against their king in 1450?

3. What part did attitudes and beliefs play in the difficulties that Henry VI faced as king?

EXAM TIP

It may be helpful to look at causes for question 1, motives and choice of action in question 2, and expectations of a king in question 3.

Summary: the role and nature of historical explanation

■ Historical explanation tries to make sense of what happened so that we can understand it. It could be described as the mortar that holds the bricks together in a coherent and recognisable design.

■ It is achieved by asking questions about the 'facts', drawing out their implications (that is, what the facts suggest) and making them explicit as part of an answer.

■ It requires us to look at different aspects of what happened, e.g. at events and situations that occurred without any planning by individuals, at the actions that such individuals took in response, and at the underlying beliefs and attitudes that they held.

■ Explanations are based on facts, but they are not factual – they arise from a choice of questions, inferences and interpretations by the historian. They are therefore hypotheses, in need of testing, support and development, and always open to further challenge, and to rejection or to refinement and consolidation.

Modes of historical explanation

Like any skilled tradesperson, historians have to use the right tools for the job. Different kinds of 'facts' need different methods, or modes, of explanation. The methods employed are defined by the nature of the task, that is, what needs to be explained:

■ Events and situations – casual mode

■ Actions – intentional mode

■ Ideas – empathetic mode.

Below we look at each of the modes. (Chapter 2 considers how the modes interact.)

Causal explanations of events and situations

In historical terms, an event is simply something that happened. A situation is a state of affairs that existed at a particular time. Events can be single and simple, such as the execution of Mary, Queen of Scots, taking place on a single day; or they can be complex, like the 1905 Revolution in Russia, which continued for most of the year. Complex events can also develop into lasting situations or 'states of affairs' such as the weakness of the Russian government in the early twentieth century. In all of these cases, historians seeking an explanation need to employ a **causal mode**. To do this, they begin with the question 'Why?' and then analyse what happened to establish causes, or causal factors. Any event can be investigated in this way.

The story of Mr Brown's car crash

Mr Brown was a busy man. He worked long hours running a small business, and his wife often complained. To please her, he promised to take her away for the weekend of their wedding anniversary. As the anniversary approached, he had been particularly hard-pressed, and did not have time to get his car serviced and a worn tyre replaced. That Friday night he was late leaving work, he was tired, and to make matters worse, it was raining. Mr Brown drove home as fast as he could, but as he turned into the road where he lived, his neighbour's dog ran across the road. Mr Brown braked hard, skidded, and crashed into a gatepost. He was not hurt, but his car was.

Why did Mr Brown's car crash?

What factors could explain the event?

Most events have more than one cause, which is why the idea of causal factors is useful. A factor can be a single item, for example the dog, or it can be a collection of items grouped around a theme, like 'pressure of work'. It is also useful to think in terms of whether a factor was a *direct* cause of the accident, or an *indirect* cause, like not getting the tyre fixed. You can set these out in a list, but it is often more helpful to set the factors out as a diagram, using arrows to show links to the outcome and to each other. This sets you thinking of causation as an active process, with each factor playing a particular part.

In the case of Mr Brown, we can identify the key factors as shown in Figure 1.2. The phrases extracted from the account show the key factors, and the arrows indicate how they linked up to cause the crash. Notice that there are lots of different links, and some arrows go directly to the crash while others go to different factors. The direct causes of the crash were the rain, the dog, Mr Brown driving fast and the worn tyre. The rain and the dog are not linked to anything else, but notice how many of the other factors all arise from the basic problem of Mr Brown's long hours. These can be seen as underlying factors.

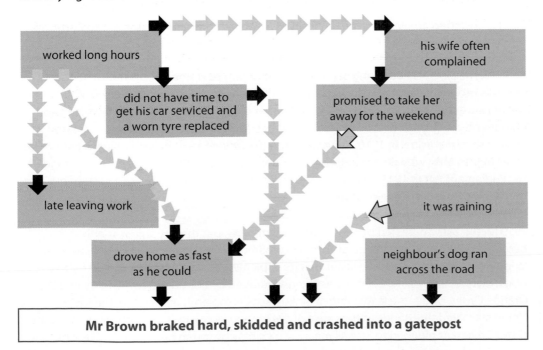

▌ Figure 1.2 The causes of Mr Brown's car crash

ACTIVITY

The story of Mr Brown's crash has now been analysed into causal factors. To establish an explanation of what happened, you could rewrite it, starting with the diagram in Figure 1.2 and explaining the links to show why Mr Brown's car crashed.

This offers a basic method for explaining why things happened, as almost anything can be treated as an event or situation. The causal mode of explanation can be applied very widely. In fact, a very good approach to historical explanation is to establish a basic causal explanation, then investigate the role of individuals within it by considering their actions and ideas, to take the explanation further. We will look more carefully at this in Chapter 2.

Explaining historical events

Most historical events have more complex causes than Mr Brown's car crash, even when the events themselves are simple. For example, the execution of Mary, Queen of Scots in 1587 arose from a number of interacting factors, which are outlined in the account below.

Mary's French upbringing and Catholic religion made it difficult for her to govern the Protestant Scots. Her relationships with Darnley and Bothwell led to her exile in England, where the English political situation and religious conflicts meant that she was a threat to Elizabeth and had to be kept in comfortable captivity away from the centre of affairs. Even so, it took her involvement in various plots against Elizabeth over a period of 20 years, and covert manipulation by some of Elizabeth's advisers to bring about Mary's trial and then her execution in 1587.

Each of these factors played a particular part in causing that event. To construct an explanation of it, you would need to consider each factor and show what it contributed to the outcome and how it linked up with other factors.

To illustrate this process, we can consider an event such as the Partition of Ireland in 1921–22. The account below describes how this event came about.

Read it and then analyse the information to establish the main causes of the Partition.

By 1912, the Liberals had a long-standing commitment to Home Rule as the solution to Ireland's problems, but the issue had divided the party and had helped to keep the Liberals out of power between 1895 and 1906. With other pressing matters such as poverty, trade unions and the growth of the Labour Party to occupy ministers, there was every reason to leave Irish issues aside. In 1910, however, Asquith's government became dependent on the votes of Irish MPs, who demanded Home Rule as the price of their support. The passage of the Parliament Act in 1911 meant that the Lords could no longer exercise a veto, and a third Home Rule Bill became inevitable.

In 1912, the Bill was passed by the House of Commons, but the struggle was only beginning. Predictably, a House of Lords dominated by Conservative Unionists and Irish landowners rejected it, which meant that its implementation would be delayed for two years. Meanwhile, resistance in Ulster was encouraged by the Conservative Party and the Orange Order. Under the leadership of Sir Edward Carson and James Craig, the Ulster Unionists rallied thousands to the cause of preventing Home Rule. In September 1912, the Ulster Covenant pledged to 'use all means which may be found necessary' to prevent

---

THINK LIKE AN HISTORIAN

Re-read the passage about Mary, Queen of Scots and underline or highlight what you consider to be causal factors. Then decide what each factor did to cause the execution.

The passage about Mary, Queen of Scots may be printed out from the CD-ROM.

Which factors were direct causes? What part did the other factors play?

Construct a diagram to show how the different factors worked together. If you wish, refer to the causal explanation diagram of Mr Brown's car crash (Figure 1.2).

CAUSAL MODE OF EXPLANATION

– the Partition of Ireland, 1921–22

Home Rule, and was signed by over 237,000 Ulstermen. The implied threat of violence was strengthened by a campaign to drive Catholics out of employment, especially in the Belfast docks, and by the open stockpiling of weapons. The nationalists of the Irish Republican Brotherhood (IRB) began to do the same, and by 1914 Ireland was on the brink of civil war.

To some extent, this was the fault of the government, and of Asquith in particular. He adopted a waiting policy in response to the Lords' rejection of the bill, which allowed the problems to get out of hand, and his belated attempts to negotiate an opt-out for Ulster came too little, too late. However, many problems were beyond his control. The Unionists had the support of the Conservative establishment, and the assertion made by Bonar Law, the leader of the Conservative Party, that 'Ulster will fight and Ulster will be right' was an echo of Lord Randolph Churchill's recommendation to 'play the Orange card' and threaten rebellion. The Curragh Mutiny, where a number of British officers threatened to leave the army rather than force Home Rule in Ulster, showed that the government could not necessarily rely on its own forces if rebellion broke out. In those circumstances the outbreak of war in 1914 offered a convenient way out, by allowing the implementation of Home Rule to be suspended for the duration of hostilities.

By the time the war ended in 1918–19, the whole situation had changed. Ulstermen fought bravely in the Great War, most famously at Thiepval on the Somme in 1916, making any abandonment of Ulster unthinkable. More importantly, Home Rule was no longer a satisfactory solution for most Irish nationalists. In 1916, an IRB rising in Dublin was brutally suppressed by the British army, and the execution of its ringleaders catastrophically mishandled. Arrested, imprisoned, tried in secret and condemned to death, their executions over several weeks were described by observers in Dublin as 'like watching a tide of blood seeping under the prison doors'. The rising had been a military fiasco, watched with indifference or impatience by most citizens of Dublin, but the combination of British mishandling and nationalist propaganda turned it into a nationalist victory. In 1918, this change in public attitudes was confirmed when Sinn Fein won a clear majority of Irish parliamentary seats and assembled in their own separate Dail (parliament) to declare Irish independence. Meanwhile, the majority in Ulster returned solidly Unionist MPs. Although it required three more years of negotiation, violence and civil war to finalise the details of the division, it was already clear that British rule was unsustainable in most of Ireland, and that partition was the only viable alternative.

The above account is a narrative of what happened, but it also contains information about why these events resulted in Partition. It therefore offers the basis of an explanation. You should begin, as with Mr Brown's car crash, by trying to define a number of causal factors. One way to approach this is by asking a series of questions that work backwards from the event.

Let's start by asking 'Why had Partition become the "only viable alternative" by 1921?' This would lead to a focus on:

- the desire of the majority for independence by 1918
- the determination of Ulster to stay within the Union.

This, in turn, would prompt a question about Irish attitudes such as 'Why did so many Irish people want independence?', which highlights:

- the importance of the 1916 Easter Rising
- the role of the IRB.

THINK LIKE AN HISTORIAN

When analysing an account, to draw out causes, think about what is suggested or implied, as well as what is actually stated. This is called inference and you need to consider it when dealing with any kind of source, if you are to understand its full value.

However, these events only occurred because: Home Rule had been delayed in 1912 and not implemented in 1914.

These issues then raise new questions about changing attitudes and the reasons for them, some of which can be answered from the account earlier, while others suggest the need for further research. The information provided here allows you to suggest an hypothesis that explains why Partition occurred, which can be tested and developed in the light of further reading.

THINK LIKE AN HISTORIAN

How far do you agree with the suggested hypothesis?

What new questions would you wish to ask about this? What areas would you suggest for further research?

Suggested hypothesis:

The Partition of Ireland in 1921 was caused by the failure of the Liberals to implement Home Rule before 1914, the impact of the Great War and British mishandling of the Easter Rising in 1916.

The hypothesis is constructed from the causal factors as a working model, a basis from which a better version can be developed. Historians would then raise further questions and use them to carry out more research. Then, in the light of that research the working hypothesis could be developed, refined, or perhaps replaced with a better one.

To arrive at this hypothesis, we also had to consider the ways in which different causal factors work together and understand the part that each one plays in the overall process of causation. Events are caused by a range of factors, each one having a particular effect on the situation. Causal explanations of events therefore arise from a *chain of cause and effect*, over a period of time. For example, the failure of attempts to establish Home Rule by 1914 (*cause*) allowed Irish resentment to grow and divisions to get worse (*effect*). This was exploited by the IRB (*cause*) and increased by British mishandling of the Easter Rising (*cause*), creating disillusionment with British promises and a growing demand for independence (*effect*).

However, cause and effect do not necessarily work in simple straight lines. The failure of Home Rule did not lead directly to Partition – rather it created the opportunity for other factors to operate. These factors, such as the role of the IRB and reactions to the Easter Rising, were direct causes of Partition, but they arose from wider attitudes in both Ireland and Britain, and these attitudes had roots much further back in Irish and British history. In fact, these attitudes had played a large part in the failure of Home Rule in the first place. In the light of this, we need to be very explicit about the precise role played by particular factors, and to go beyond simply using them as separate 'causes'. Looking at how each factor worked and how it affected the situation at different times raises new questions, enabling us to carry out further research into the various attitudes and beliefs that were held in different parts of Ireland as well as in Britain, and then to amend the suggested hypothesis to take account of these factors. This can be illustrated by a diagram, showing how we have worked back from the final outcome to establish 'causes' – see Figure 1.3.

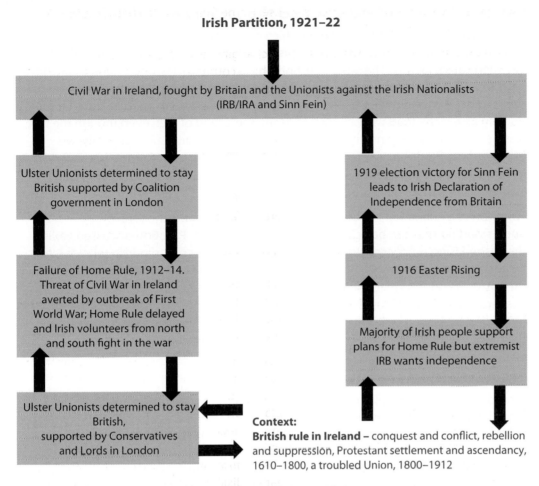

Irish Partition, 1921–22

Civil War in Ireland, fought by Britain and the Unionists against the Irish Nationalists (IRB/IRA and Sinn Fein)

Ulster Unionists determined to stay British supported by Coalition government in London

1919 election victory for Sinn Fein leads to Irish Declaration of Independence from Britain

Failure of Home Rule, 1912–14. Threat of Civil War in Ireland averted by outbreak of First World War; Home Rule delayed and Irish volunteers from north and south fight in the war

1916 Easter Rising

Ulster Unionists determined to stay British, supported by Conservatives and Lords in London

Majority of Irish people support plans for Home Rule but extremist IRB wants independence

Context:
British rule in Ireland – conquest and conflict, rebellion and suppression, Protestant settlement and ascendancy, 1610–1800, a troubled Union, 1800–1912

▌ **Figure 1.3** Working back from the final outcome to establish the causes of Irish Partition

Summary: causal explanations

It is possible to draw some conclusions about the nature of causal explanations and how they are established:

- To explain events and situations historians use a causal mode, based on a chain of cause and effect. This is done by analysing 'what happened' to establish causal factors, which can include actions and ideas as well as earlier events.

- Questions are asked to establish causal links between each factor and the final outcome, and between different factors, to establish the role of each factor in the overall process and the ways in which they worked together and interacted.

- This allows historians to produce an explanatory hypothesis and to raise new questions in order to develop it further, through research and investigation.

Before moving on to consider other types of explanation, it may be useful to apply the methodology demonstrated here to other events, in order to consolidate your understanding of it. This can be done by choosing another event from within this option – such as the reform of the House of Lords in 1911, or the granting of votes to some women in 1918 – or by moving to another option such as the French or Russian Revolution. Either way, you will need to begin by reading about what happened.

The significance of actions and the impact of individuals

The last section set out the method by which events and situations can be explained using a causal mode of explanation, that is, establishing chains of cause and effect between causal factors. The basic question was 'Why did this happen?' and all factors or parts of a situation were treated in the same way. In the case of Mr Brown's car crash, the fact that it was raining, that he wanted to keep a promise to his wife and that the dog ran across the road were all treated as the same kind of fact, even though the first was a situation, the second an attitude, and the third was an action. Similarly, we explained the Partition of Ireland by reference to the failure to establish Home Rule by 1914 (situation), the impact of the First World War (event), and the Easter Rising of 1916 – an event which can also be seen as an action carried out by the IRB.

This form of explanation is a useful starting point, but it limits the level of understanding that can be achieved. In the explanation of Partition discussed earlier, the Easter Rising is only considered in terms of its impact on Anglo-Irish relations, but an understanding of why Partition came about also requires an understanding of why the Easter Rising took place. It did not just happen but was the result of a decision and of specific actions taken by the leaders of the IRB. Therefore, to understand the situation fully, it is necessary to ask 'Why did they act in this way?' This will allow us to explore their motives and intentions as well as their impact.

Intentional explanation of actions

To address these issues, historians use the **intentional mode** of explanation. This method considers the intentions and motives that lie behind actions. Unlike events, actions are the result of conscious decisions (however pressurised, hasty or instinctive they may be) and therefore arise from some kind of intention. The key question asked by historians is therefore 'Why did X act in this way?' or 'What did X hope to achieve by this action?', and answers have to be found by investigating what X said they wanted, as well as making inferences from what they did and from what others thought they were trying to achieve.

However, the process of defining a person's intentions is not simple and rarely produces certainty. While actions may be clear and visible, the motives and intentions behind them are not. They are internal to the 'actor', who may or may not be willing to explain them honestly, and may sometimes not be entirely clear themselves why they act in a particular way. We cannot rely entirely on what people say they intended. Similarly, contemporaries may well have opinions as to what was intended – but there is always a question as to how well-informed they are, or whether they are influenced by motives and objectives of their own. Nor is it possible to judge motives from the outcomes and results of actions – there are occasions when actions produce results and reactions that are quite different to what was intended.

This can be set out in the form of a diagram that summarises the process of intentional explanation (see Figure 1.4). It does not set out a rigid method to follow, but illustrates the kind of question that can be asked to investigate intentions and explain actions.

Intentional mode

Historical method of enquiry used to explain actions by considering the intentions and

THINK LIKE AN HISTORIAN

Historians use a number of terms when referring to what people want or intend to achieve by a particular action.

- Motives – what makes people act.

- Aims – the things that they are pursuing.

- Objectives – the more precise things that they expect to reach by particular actions.

The intentional mode of explanation allows historians to define the expectations held by a person in choosing a particular action – that is, what they intended to be the result(s) of the action taken.

What is the action intended to achieve?

What action is taken?

What outcomes does the action produce?

What intentions could the 'actor' have had?

What was happening?
What was the situation before the action taken?

What does the 'actor' say they intended?
Does this seem likely given the wider situation?

Action taken

What do other people say the 'actor' intended?
How can they know?
Are they reliable witnesses?

What were the results of this action
(a) for the 'actor', and
(b) for others?

Were they the likely results, given the wider situation?
Could they have been foreseen?

How did other people react?
Did this affect the results of the action taken?

Do you need to re-evaluate?

Or Is it an example of an unintended outcome?

What happened next?
How did the situation change as a result of the action?

What further actions and reactions took place?

How did the 'actor' deal with these results?

Does this suggest that the results were expected or unexpected? If they could have been foreseen, how does this fit with the supposed intentions

▌ **Figure 1.4** The process of intentional explanation

ACTIVITY

Figure 1.4 illustrates the process of investigation involved in developing intentional explanations. To explore this for yourself, look through any current newspaper, where you will find plenty of actions reported, often accompanied by interviews and opinions that claim to explain what was happening. Examples include sporting occasions, political issues and the behaviour of 'celebrities'. Choose one that interests you. Use the questions suggested here (or others that are similar) to construct an explanation of what was done, why and with what results. Then consider:

■ Did the actions produce the results that were intended?

■ How sure can you be that your explanation is accurate?

This means that attempts to explain actions rely very much on inference and judgement, and this is a major reason why historians' opinions and explanations can differ. It is not simply a matter of 'bias' or of deliberately distorting what happened. The fact is that there are many areas where we cannot be certain of what happened and have to rely on developing a judgement based on the evidence available – and in historical situations this may be quite limited. For example, there is no guarantee that someone taking an action will ever have explained what they intended. What makes an intentional explanation useful is not the level of certainty, but the process by which it explores the issues, argues through the possibilities and develops understanding of the role and impact of individuals and their actions.

INTENTIONAL MODE OF EXPLANATION

– Martin Luther's 95 Theses, 1517

QUICK FACT

Indulgences were documents issued by the Church that claimed to be able to release souls from purgatory (where they had to suffer punishment for their sins). This applied not only to the donor, whose money was benefiting the Church, but could also be used for their dead relatives. In effect, the Church was claiming the power to draw on Christ's sacrifice and God's forgiveness to benefit those who served the Church.

QUICK FACT

The **Dominicans** were rivals to Luther's own monastic order, the Augustinians, and were closely associated with the papacy and Rome.

To illustrate these points, let's consider one of the most famous actions in western European history – the action of Martin Luther in pinning his 95 Theses to the door of the Church in Wittenberg in 1517, thereby sparking a division in the western Christian Church that never healed. The action in itself raises the obvious question: 'Why did Luther take this action?', while knowledge of its outcome raises the issue of whether this was what he intended to happen. This forms the basis of an investigation, and may give rise to a third question: 'If it was not his intention, then why did such a division arise from his action?'

Luther's *stated* intention in pinning up the theses was to initiate a debate about the problems facing the Church and in particular about the sale of **indulgences**.

This claim is supported by the fact that the theses were written in Latin (the language of scholarly debate) and that they did not directly criticise the Church or its leaders, although some of Luther's arguments already implied more fundamental differences with them. It can also be argued that, given the power and authority exercised by the Church at the time, a direct challenge would have been not only brave but also foolish. On the basis of experience, Luther could have expected to find himself in the same position as earlier reformers such as Jan Hus, another professor, whose challenge to the authority of the Church led to him being treated as a heretic and burned at the stake in 1415.

Consideration of Luther's action and the wider historical context therefore supports the argument that Luther's intentions were as he claimed and that his objective was to encourage debate, but this does not fully answer why he acted as he did. In addition to his direct intentions, historians would consider any other 'hidden' motives, and the influence of his character and experience. Luther was a scholar with extensive knowledge of the Bible, living in an age when the Church was heavily criticised for its wealth, encouragement of superstition and lax morality. These concerns had recently been highlighted by the arrival in Germany of Johann Tetzel, a **Dominican** friar authorised by the Pope to sell indulgences in order to raise money to build a new cathedral in Rome. They were also supported by the Archbishop of Mainz, who needed the money to repay debts incurred in buying his position. As such, they symbolised much of what Luther and others believed to be wrong with the Church.

The implications of what Luther wrote show that he was already moving towards an emphasis on personal faith, on the basis of the Bible, that conflicted with fundamental doctrines preached by the Church. In particular, he rejected as false teaching the idea that people could merit forgiveness of their sins by doing good deeds and he strongly condemned the practice of selling indulgences as a blatant corruption forbidden by the Church's own laws. On both counts, the people were being deceived. We also know that Luther was a man of strong convictions and hasty temper. It is therefore reasonable to suggest that while his conscious motives may have been exactly as he claimed, his underlying motives (and therefore the reasons why he acted as he did) included anger at the sale of indulgences, disgust at the corruption of leading clerics and underlying convictions about faith that were already distancing him from the mainstream Church.

By using the intentional mode of explanation, we have been able to explain Luther's action, by referring to:

- his stated intentions
- the wider historical situation
- his own character and attitudes, and
- our knowledge of the likely outcomes.

We have not, however, explained why Luther's action led to its actual outcome – the division of the western Church – because that did not arise from Luther's action alone. To pursue that enquiry we would have to consider a wider range of actions – how the Church responded to Luther, what reactions he created in Germany and how these responses impacted on Luther himself. Just as the causal mode of explanation requires consideration of a range of factors, related by chains of cause and effect, the intentional mode requires understanding of both actions and reactions, often over a period of time. We might also find that considering actions alone would not be sufficient, and that we would need to set them in the context of the wider historical situation and the attitudes and beliefs held at the time.

THINK LIKE AN HISTORIAN

As we saw earlier, historians do not see causation as a series of separately linked items but as a complex process, often developing over a period of time. Just as we considered chains of cause and effect as part of the causal mode of explanation, so chains of action and reaction provide a structure for intentional explanation.

A chain of action and reaction may involve a two-way relationship, but more often the interaction of two individuals or groups is affected by external factors, including the actions of others and the impact of events and situations. The explanation offered here of Luther's actions demonstrates a basic technique, but the explanation of major developments in history usually requires a wide range of factors to be considered, and the use of more than one explanatory mode. (This is illustrated in Chapter 2 Building historical explanations, where there is a further investigation of Luther's role and impact.)

The chain of action and reaction can be examined more fully by considering an example from France in 1789. In May, the king met with the **Estates-General** in order to develop a programme of reform and deal with the financial crisis that had paralysed government since 1787. Instead, the meeting produced popular unrest and intervention, and the beginnings of revolution. The following extracts (adapted from *The French Revolution* by Lucille Kekewich and Susan Rose) trace a series of decisions and actions that explain why the situation changed.

Source ③

The Third Estate contained an overwhelming majority of lawyers, [and] a large group of royal office holders, most of whom came from towns and from the north of France. All would have seen themselves as educated men familiar with the questions that had been so vigorously debated all winter… Now that the majority of these deputies had actually gathered at Versailles their initial feelings were largely of frustration. The King's speech at the opening session on 5 May had been bland and non-committal. Necker [the king's financial adviser] spoke for more than three hours on the state of the nation's finances with no sign of a plan of action. The apparently technical issue of verifying the deputies' credentials reflected the still undecided issue of whether the Estates should vote by head or by Estate. The outcome of this would decide whether there was any chance of the Third Estate achieving dominance, now that its total number of deputies outnumbered those of the other two combined.

On 17 June the Third Estate, prompted by the Abbe Sieyes, voted by 491 votes to 90 to adopt the title of National Assembly. The vote challenged the other two estates to join their supposed inferiors in representing the people of France. The assembly of the clergy (First Estate) which contained a large

QUICK FACT

The **Estates-General** was an assembly of representatives of the French people, a little (but only a little) like a parliament. It did not represent individuals, but 'estates' or classes – the clergy, the nobility, and the commoners (mainly the middle classes). The different Estates met separately and voted on issues as an Estate, so that any decisions would be simply made by a 2–1 majority. The king did not have to listen to it, but the fact that it was called suggested a desire to hear what 'the people' wanted and gain support for reforms. The last time the Estates-General had been called before 1789 was in 1614, so its meeting was very significant.

CHAIN OF ACTION AND REACTION

– the French Revolution, 1789

What does this paragraph suggest about the initial intentions of (a) the king and his ministers, and (b) the members of the Third Estate, when they met in May 1789?

How far do these actions suggest that the intentions of the Third Estate were changing? What reasons are indicated?

How far was the growing conflict caused by the actions of the king? How did the deputies react? Were these reactions always what was expected or intended by the king?

Did the people of Paris take action in order to create 'a new political balance'?

Did the king's appearance in Paris suggest that his intentions had changed?

QUICK FACT

The **Bastille** was an old royal fortress in the middle of Paris, used as an arsenal and sometimes as a prison for those who displeased the king. People could be imprisoned without trial, by a *lettre de cachet*, which was simply a warrant signed by the king. The fortress was therefore a symbol of royal authority, perhaps tyranny, and although the popular attack on it was probably a mixture of self-defence and an attempt to seize weapons, its fall came to symbolise the collapse of the absolute monarchy and the old regime.

Source ③ Continued

majority of deputies from the lower clergy, voted two days later to join this national assembly, and were followed by some of the well-known liberal nobles over the next few days. At Court the King's more thoughtful advisers, including Necker, could see that the situation threatened to get out of hand. The King himself (never the most forceful of characters and still suffering from the recent death of his much-loved eldest son) agreed under pressure to hold a Royal Session on 23 June, where at last an authoritative reform programme would be presented. Despite the intervention of the Queen and the Comte d'Artois (Louis' younger brother) to make this programme more rigid and less attractive to the reformers, this did constitute a significant step forward.

Before the Session could take place some alterations were necessary to the meeting-place of the National Assembly. The doors were locked and soldiers stationed outside. No one had bothered to warn the deputies of these plans, and on the morning of 20 June they found their access barred. In a state of great excitement they moved to the nearest suitable alternative hall – the King's Tennis Court – and there swore the oath never to disperse until their work of reforming the constitution was complete. On 23 June the King came to address the deputies in this atmosphere of mounting tension and suspicion. His speech contained a number of reform proposals, which might have been acceptable if put forward by Necker on 5 May, but it had been overtaken by events. In particular, the King's refusal

to accept the validity of the vote of 17 June establishing the National Assembly swung opinion against him. The deputies refused to disperse as requested.

By early July Paris was in ferment, with opposition meetings and discussions centred on the Palais Royal, the residence of the apparently liberal Duc d'Orleans, the king's cousin. As a matter of deliberate royal policy the number of troops stationed in the Paris area was increasing rapidly, with troops drawn largely from foreign mercenary regiments since the loyalty of some French regiments was suspect. On 11 July Necker was abruptly dismissed by the King, thus confirming in the minds of many Parisians all the rumours that had been circulating concerning the desire of the King to arrest members of the National Assembly and halt the move to reform. Paris was soon in turmoil, with large crowds in the streets and rumours of an attack. In search of arms they congregated at the Bastille, where they were fired upon from the walls before the arrival of deserting soldiers and their artillery forced the governor, de Launay, to surrender the fortress.

Thereafter unrest spread quickly. The King restored Necker to office, and himself appeared in Paris on 17 July. He wore the red, white and blue flag of the revolution in a gesture that did little to restore his reputation but said much about the power of the Parisians and a new political balance.

Adapted from Kekewich, L. and Rose, S. (1990) The French Revolution, Longman.

THINK LIKE AN HISTORIAN

List the key actions taken by the king, the Third Estate and the people of Paris. Then trace how the actions of one and the reactions of others led to 'a new political balance' in France. You should also consider accidental or unintended outcomes to particular actions. You could do this in writing or by using a diagram. Then use the material to offer a brief answer to the question: Why did Louis XVI's attempt to reform France lead instead to revolution?

Summary: intentional mode of explanation

Historical explanation needs to do more than consider a sequence of events. The role and impact of individuals and particular groups on historical situations and developments is significant, and can only be understood by an investigation of their actions. To do this, historians use an intentional mode of explanation, in which they consider the intentions and objectives that lead to actions as well as the outcomes and reactions that they generate. This applies to unintentional outcomes as well those that are planned – indeed, it could be argued that many key historical events and developments arise from the mistakes and misjudgements of those involved rather than the intended consequences of their actions.

Therefore, an intentional explanation requires:

- the use of key questions such as: 'Why did X act in this way?', 'What were their intentions or objectives?', 'What did they hope to achieve by…?'

- awareness that while actions can be seen, intentions and objectives can only be inferred, that they may be disguised or subconscious, and that they may change with changing circumstances

- analysis of outcomes, both intended and unintended, to assess their impact on different situations and explain the developments that arise

- understanding that outcomes may arise from a chain of actions and reactions, and that complex explanations require understanding of interaction between individuals and the circumstances in which they act.

The importance of ideas

The 'circumstances in which people act' include events and wider situations, as well as the effect of actions taken by others, but equal importance must be attached to the impact of **ideas**. The term does not relate to individual feelings and priorities, but rather to the general attitudes and beliefs (sometimes called values, or **value systems**) that existed within a particular society or section of it. Historians are not seeking to understand 'how people felt', which is probably impossible, but they do need to understand the attitudes and beliefs that they characteristically shared in any particular period, because 'ideas' influence both actions and events.

The most direct impact of ideas tends to be through influencing the actions and reactions of individuals and groups within a society. Ideas therefore play a large part in shaping interaction, for example between Luther and the Church or between Louis XVI, the deputies of the Third Estate and the people of Paris. However, ideas also influence the way that people respond to events and situations, because they affect the way that we interpret them, how seriously we take them and what we see as remedies. For example, plague epidemics in medieval and early modern Europe were seen by many as a punishment from God; the threat of a flu epidemic in modern Britain is blamed on the government for failing to stockpile sufficient vaccine.

The importance of beliefs and values can be illustrated by the way that leaders of the Church responded to Luther's actions in 1517. They mishandled Luther's challenge because:

- as leaders of a Church that was also a political institution, they were preoccupied with political issues such as the forthcoming election of a new Holy Roman Emperor

- they saw nothing wrong with using the spiritual power of the Church to raise money for its physical glorification

- their ideas about the authority of the Church encouraged them to assume that an obscure German professor could be silenced by skilled intellectuals who held superior status within it

- their ideas about God and salvation encouraged them to believe that, if necessary, the threat of **excommunication** was all that was needed to terrify Luther into giving up his ideas, as it had many others in the past.

Ideas

The term **ideas** is used to refer to the beliefs and values that relate to a particular society and shape the attitudes and expectations that influence those who live in it. While historians take into account the influence of universally held human attitudes – affection, greed and an instinct for survival and self-preservation, for example – they also consider the impact of value systems that are characteristic of different periods and cultures and help to influence the actions

IMPORTANCE OF BELIEFS AND VALUES

– Martin Luther's 95 Theses, 1517

QUICK FACTS

Excommunication meant that an individual would be excluded from the Church and its services, both spiritual and social. Given the role of the Church in everyday life, this meant almost total isolation, or worse. More importantly, according to Catholic beliefs, the Church represented the only path to God and salvation – so excommunication was also a denial of entry to heaven and a sentence of eternal damnation in the fires of hell.

A Diet (nothing to do with eating!) was the name given to a meeting of all the German princes to make important political decisions. Germany at this time was not a single country but a collection of small states governed in theory by the Holy Roman Emperor, a title first adopted by Charlemagne in 800 CE. In this system, each prince governed his own small state, and met with others at different places when summoned by the emperor, to discuss important problems. The problem of Luther was discussed in 1521 in the city of Worms – the **Diet of Worms** – where the Emperor Charles declared Luther an outlaw, banned him from the empire and demanded that he be arrested on sight. Fortunately for Luther, some of the German princes ignored the ban and it was never enforced.

Because of these attitudes, Church leaders reacted slowly to Luther's challenge between 1517 and 1521, giving him time to develop his ideas and gather support, and when decisive action was attempted after the **Diet of Worms** in 1521, Luther's supporters were able to protect him.

THINK LIKE AN HISTORIAN

The example of Luther illustrates the role and importance of ideas and attitudes in shaping actions and interaction. Using this as a guide, re-read source 4, an account of the early stages of the revolution in France, and suggest ways in which ideas and attitudes influenced the actions of both the king and his opposition, and influenced the growth of a radical challenge to royal authority. Alternatively, you could consider a current situation or a recent action/event and apply the same process to the role of ideas by addressing the ideas that helped to cause it, or those that influence different responses to it. In either case, be careful to focus on underlying attitudes rather than particular aims or intentions.

Empathetic explanation of ideas

The role and influence of ideas means that a full explanation of any historical situation or development must include an explanation of the beliefs that influenced and shaped it. Some historical events, such as the twelfth-century Crusades, the European Reformation and the twentieth-century Cold War, have been described as primarily conflicts of ideas, although these claims can be, and have been, challenged.

However, ideas cannot be explained in the same way as events or actions. They did not just 'happen' and they were often not intentionally created. Some individuals may well have sought to highlight or develop particular ideas, for particular purposes, but to be widely accepted and influential, the arguments and claims made about them must fit with the underlying assumptions and attitudes that people hold at the time.

It is important to distinguish between versions of an idea, that is, the philosophical writings that present, publicise or amend particular ideas and beliefs, and the 'idea' itself. Works such as Luther's *On the Liberty of a Christian Man* (1520), Rousseau's *Social Contract* (1762), and Karl Marx's *Communist Manifesto* (1848) are part of the development of ideas and serve as examples for analysis and discussion, but the act of creating and publishing them requires an intentional explanation. The ideas themselves need to be explained by reference to what they involved, where they came from and how they related to the wider economic, social, political and cultural characteristics of the period in which they existed. For this, we need to offer an **empathetic explanation** based on the nature, origins, development and appeal of the ideas that define attitudes and beliefs.

In order to understand an idea, it is necessary to define its main features (not always a simple task!) and consider where it came from and how it developed. This may well involve exploring its roots and origins in earlier ideas, as well as tracing its development through the actions of individuals and impact of events. It is also important to understand the idea's appeal within the historical context – why it was widely accepted at the time. For example, to understand the European Reformation, we need to explain the nature of Protestant beliefs and why they were sufficiently appropriate to the time to attract widespread support. This involves:

- analysing Luther's ideas about salvation by faith alone and the authority of the Bible to understand and develop their implications

- relating the ideas to earlier Christian sources and the ideas of earlier reformers like Hus and Wycliffe

- investigating the state of the Church and society to see why the ideas might have a particular appeal at this time

- exploring how Luther's ideas were shaped by his conflict with the Church and his need for political support

- assessing the appeal of Luther's teachings to secular rulers (city magistrates and territorial princes)

- evaluating why his ideas spread so far and so fast (unlike the teachings of any previous religious leader,

- (probably) considering how the contribution of other reformers like Zwingli and Calvin, as well as their interaction with Luther, influenced later developments.

In the process, we will touch on many of the same events and situations as those that we addressed earlier in explaining Luther's actions. The difference would lie in the focus of the enquiry, the questions asked about such events and therefore the answers that would be obtained. This is the case with the examples below, which introduce and explain some of the key ideas that have influenced historical development in western Europe.

> **Empathetic explanation**
>
> Historical method of enquiry used to explain the nature, origins, development and appeal of ideas that

THINK LIKE AN HISTORIAN

The methods used by historians to investigate the past can appear remarkably similar to those used by police and reputable journalists, for example, to investigate the present. In both cases, the enquiry considers actions and events by asking the kind of questions posed earlier in the chapter, considering motives and exploring the attitudes that help to shape them. Quite often, these investigations pay little attention to ideas and beliefs because, being contemporary, they are assumed to be familiar (although this is not always the case).

In studying the past, historians cannot make these assumptions – the attitudes and beliefs that are characteristic of an historical period are an important part of it, and may well differ from those of the historian. To develop historical understanding of an issue, it is necessary to investigate the nature of attitudes and beliefs, and why they seemed appropriate or were influential at that particular time. Ideas rarely exist in isolation, and historians need to consider how ideas relate to other aspects of life, as well as the role that they played in shaping historical development.

Example 1: The role and impact of ideas during the French Revolution

The early months of the French Revolution as described earlier offer a good example of the need to understand and explain ideas. While many of Louis' problems arose from his indecisive character and the actions of others such as Marie Antoinette, it is increasingly clear from source 3 on pages – 16 that there was a significant difference between his attitudes and beliefs and those of the Third Estate. Louis had been brought up and trained for kingship in a system of Divine Right monarchy (see below), while members of the Third Estate had been increasingly influenced by the ideas of the eighteenth-century Enlightenment (see below).

ACTIVITY

Re-read source 3 and then the empathetic explanation offered below, in order to explain how the influence of conflicting ideas contributed to the growing tension that undermined the efforts of Louis XVI to reform the existing system of government. (See Exam Tip for guidance.)

> **EXAM TIP**
>
> You may find it useful to begin the activity by producing a table to relate particular actions and intentions to the beliefs held by the actors. List the actions taken, and in each case consider: 'What was this intended to achieve?' and 'What does this suggest about underlying beliefs and ideas?'. Alternatively, you can list what happened as events, and then use the ideas to explain how each party interpreted these events, what they expected to happen, and how these different interpretations caused problems between them. You can use source 4 to compile your list, then read the empathetic explanation on page 20 to identify the relevant ideas.

EMPATHETIC EXPLANATION

– Divine Right and the Enlightenment

Where did ideas of Divine Right come from?

The theory of Divine Right claimed that kings were appointed by God, through a system of inheritance (heredity) and were responsible only to God for their actions. The idea had a long history, dating back to the Roman Empire. In 800 CE, when Charlemagne sought to establish his Frankish Empire on a more permanent foundation, he accepted coronation as emperor from the Pope in Rome, which emphasised his inheritance of Roman tradition and his close relationship with the Church. Similarly, when the Russian rulers took control after the Mongol invasions, they adopted the title of Tsar (derived from the word Caesar) and claimed the backing of God through coronation by the church.

Throughout the medieval period, the system became more formalised, with an increasing emphasis on inheritance by the eldest son. It reached its height in the west in the late seventeenth century under Louis XIV in France, who claimed sufficient power to subordinate not only the nobility and people to his will, but to some extent, the Church as well.

Why were such ideas widely accepted and for so long? In the first place, Divine Right did not mean that a king could do as he liked. He made the law, but he was also expected to live within it and apply it justly, unless exceptional circumstances decreed otherwise. He expected obedience from his subjects, but in return he had a duty to provide protection. He was responsible to God – and therefore limited by the religious code and values that underpinned his power and were often (certainly in the case of Louis XVI) a matter of sincere belief for the king himself. This distinguishes Divine Right absolutism from crude tyranny, but it also emphasises the main reason for acceptance of the Divine Right of kings – the majority of people at the time believed in a God who controlled the affairs of men, and indeed the workings of nature. Since God was the key to understanding the universe, it was not surprising that the idea of a God-given hierarchy among men, as in nature, should be widely understood and believed.

In what ways were ideas about Divine Right appropriate for the time?

Why were they widely accepted?

Not only did the Church reinforce this concept of hierarchical authority as ordained by God, it was also considered to be essential to good order. Most of the states where Divine Right monarchy became established had experienced periods of civil war and threats of invasion – the need for an authority that could command obedience and ensure protection mattered far more than the rights of individuals who might threaten it. It is no coincidence that the concept declined first in England, protected by the sea and surrounded by weaker kingdoms, and last in the vast hinterland of Russia, where distance and a lack of natural boundaries made invasion and upheaval a constant threat.

What were the main features of the Enlightenment?

How did these ideas develop?

By the late eighteenth century, these assumptions were being challenged for a number of reasons. The example of England played a part, for the abandonment of Divine Right in favour of a parliamentary monarchy by the end of the seventeenth century had allowed the government to tap into national resources on an unheard-of scale, and initiated a period of economic and imperial expansion. This coincided with a scientific revolution that challenged old certainties, emphasised the importance of reason and practical benefits, and came to be known as the Enlightenment. By the late eighteenth century, the influence of these ideas had spread beyond 'science' to apply scientific thought and methods to a range of human activities, including politics. Where Montesquieu had praised the English system of government because it was practical and effective, Rousseau's Social Contract claimed to set out universal principles based on scientific research and the application of rational thought. More importantly (and, ironically, since early scientists like Newton had been motivated by a desire to understand the universe that they believed God had created), the new thinking challenged the power of religion. Only a few of the new philosophers, like Voltaire, ever denied the existence of God, but most argued that, just as the universe operated by its own natural laws, so should the affairs of men. God might have created them, but he did not directly interfere in their workings. With this, the basis of Divine Right monarchy disappeared, and the search for a better system, based on natural law and justice took its place.

THINK LIKE AN HISTORIAN

The above account traces the development of two influential political ideas: the basis for Divine Right monarchy and its replacement by a more democratic system. Ideas about the precise form of that replacement varied, and few at the time saw anything like a modern democracy, with or without a monarchy.

The 'ideas' that are being considered here are not fully worked-out schemes of government but are underlying principles that would guide and inform attempts to find systems that would suit a particular time and place. As such, two key features are apparent:

- The ideas evolved slowly, over a long period of time.

- The ideas grew naturally from existing ideas, experience, and changing situations.

As mentioned earlier, it is important to distinguish between particular versions of an idea, which are often deliberately and consciously created, and the underlying assumptions and attitudes that shape and create them.

The revolutionary legacy

It is widely accepted that the upheavals that broke out in France in 1789 were not deliberately planned as a **revolution**, involving the violent destruction of the old regime and its replacement by something very different. However, part of its legacy was the establishment of the idea of revolution as something to be sought and worked towards. Revolution as a means of achieving political (and possibly social, economic and cultural) change was an idea that divided Europe throughout the nineteenth century. On the one hand, the restored monarchs and their allies after 1815 were terrified of the possibility; on the other, the more radical reformers among their subjects regarded it as a legitimate tool for achieving change, and some worked for it both actively and consciously.

Revolutionary activity took many forms, but before 1848 most were primarily concerned with political change and the creation of new systems of government. However, the nineteenth century also saw economic and social developments through an industrial 'revolution' that gradually transformed society and the relationships within it. Increasingly, some reformers argued that political revolution was not enough, and that governments should take responsibility for the social and economic needs of the people. Without adequate provision for their material needs, claims to equality were false and political freedom was meaningless. By the late nineteenth century, these ideas – whether reformist or revolutionary – were generally labelled **socialist**.

Example 2: Revolution in Russia

Socialism, in one form or another, has been one of the dominant ideas of the twentieth century. The most widely recognised version of socialism was created by Karl Marx in the mid-nineteenth century. It was particularly coherent, and because it envisaged a revolution that would take control of the state and exercise power in government, it appeared to promise the greatest success. It also claimed to have the force of history behind it, because it was based on a **historical dialectic** (see page 22), or conflict of opposing forces that showed an inevitable socialist victory, as shown in Figure 1.5. This illustration is taken from a school textbook, published in 1988. It attempts to summarise the ideas of Karl Marx about how society had evolved and how it would move towards socialism and the 'Just Society'. This came to be known as the **Marxist dialectic** (see page 22). As the illustration shows, Marx argued that each economic system contained the seeds of change and the source of the next phase.

Revolution and socialist

Few terms are more difficult to define effectively than **revolution**, but **socialist** is certainly one of them.

Historians generally accept that revolution relates to change through violent upheaval as opposed to more gradual reform, but the term is often used less precisely, and there is still considerable debate as to which historical events merit use of the term.

The term socialist has been used to describe a wide range of ideas and individuals (sometimes as a term of abuse) and is often used interchangeably with communist and Marxist. The last is incorrect. Marxism, the idea that the state would inevitably be taken over by the working-classes to create a genuinely cooperative and equal society, was one form of socialism that became particularly dominant by the late nineteenth century, but it was never the only source of socialist ideas and plans.

The French socialists St Simon (who advocated strong government control to ensure social and economic equality) and Fourier (who argued that society should be organised in small independent communities) both pre-dated Marx. Marx himself gave very precise definitions of both socialism and communism, as stages on the road to a 'just society'. In common useage, the term socialist has tended to be used to cover a broad range of ideas of the left, concerned with society as a whole rather than separate individuals. The term communist has particular associations with Marxism as interpreted in Soviet Russia.

2 Building historical explanations

Introduction

In Chapter 1, we learned that historical situations and developments arise from a combination of ideas, actions and events, and that these different types of occurrences require different modes of explanation. The chapter also showed that no single mode of explanation is sufficient in itself, because ideas, actions and events work together and interact to create outcomes and developments. The key to building good historical explanations is an understanding of this process of interaction.

This can be illustrated by returning to the relatively simple example of Mr Brown's car crash – if you need to refresh your memory, see Chapter 1 The nature of historical explanation, page 6. The crash involved a combination of ideas, actions and events. The basic problem was Mr Brown's habitual *action* of working long hours, which affected his relationship with his wife. He therefore promised her a weekend away, which suggests an *intention* to please her *based on the idea* that his marriage was important. When he found himself late once more, this led him into the *action* of driving fast, which was unfortunate when his long hours had also prevented him from taking care of his car. All this put Mr Brown at risk that night, but it did not make the crash inevitable. Two *events* that Mr Brown could not control – the rain and the dog in the road – were necessary to cause him to brake hard, and this linked with his speed and the worn tyre (and possibly the fact that he was tired) to bring about the crash. It only happened when all the factors combined and interacted at a particular moment.

This brief account also illustrates that causation is a process that develops over time. Some of the *factors* had existed for some time – the habit of working long hours, the problems in Mr Brown's marriage and the state of the car and tyre. These did not make an accident inevitable, but they did gradually build up a situation, or conditions, in which it became increasingly likely. Historians describe these as **conditional factors** – they make an outcome possible and increasingly probable, or likely to happen. However, for the outcome to finally take place, there have to be other factors that trigger it, and influence the timing, the way it happens, and sometimes how serious it is. These are known as contingencies, or **contingent factors**. For Mr Brown, these were the rain, the dog and his speed. Most historical events arise from the interaction of conditional and contingent factors, which usually involve a combination of ideas, actions and events. Historical explanations are built up by identifying and linking these different elements, using the appropriate mode to explain each one and explicit links to demonstrate their part in the overall process.

At that stage, the process becomes more complicated. It is relatively easy to show that a range of factors plays *some* part in the process of causation, but evaluating precisely what part is a matter of judgement, relying on inference rather than knowledge. To develop an explanation fully, historians need to *analyse* the process that they are explaining, *evaluate* the role and importance of different factors, and *synthesise* their judgements into an overall conclusion. The basis of all this is their understanding of interaction. Only when they have reached an understanding of how factors interacted to cause something can they begin to make judgements about the part played by any one factor, its relationship to other factors, and therefore its relative importance.

MODES OF EXPLANATION

Need to refresh your memory?

- Causal mode
  see page 6

- Intentional mode
  see page 12

- Empathetic mode
  see page 18

THINK LIKE AN HISTORIAN

Relative importance or significance

The importance of particular factors is addressed in different ways. Historians often attribute significance to particular events, actions and ideas, when explaining both causation and change over time. This means looking at the effects of a particular occurrence (both short and long term) and deciding that they had some significant effect on a particular situation. It can be approached by looking at occurrences as single items.

When historians begin to address the importance of factors within a process, however, they have to consider their importance in relation to the whole. That means making judgements about how important a particular factor was compared to (in relation to) other factors. That kind of judgement cannot just be stated; it has to be argued through by explaining the role and interaction of different factors. Such claims are only judgements, however persuasive. This is one reason why all historical explanations are conditional, and open to debate.

How modes of explanation interact

The case studies that follow will show you the range of tools that can be used for these tasks and the ways in which they can be applied. The material in the sources is deliberately limited because you are learning how to build explanations rather than studying a period of history in depth. You will be able to find out more about the examples that relate to your chosen options when you begin to focus on them in your course of study. Meanwhile, you are not expected to have background knowledge, and you should find the material provided here sufficient for the tasks and activities that are suggested. Case studies 1–3 build on the separate modes of explanation described in Chapter 1, to show how one mode invokes another and how an explanation is built up. This demonstrates interaction between factors. However, the final section takes this further, showing how this interaction can be analysed and developed to enable judgements to be made about relative importance.

Case study 1: The Partition of Ireland

In Chapter 1, we established a brief causal explanation of why Ireland was partitioned in 1921–22, and offered a hypothesis for further investigation (see page 10). Both were very limited, because we focused on explaining the causes of an event, and actions and ideas were only addressed within that framework. However, their nature and impact as factors within the explanation raise other questions, which need to be explored using different modes of explanation. The sources and explanation on pages 8–11 highlighted the failure of the Liberals to implement Home Rule in 1914 as a key conditional factor causing partition. This was caused by events like the signing of the Ulster Covenant and the Curragh Mutiny, but in order to understand fully what was going on, it may be useful to consider these as actions and investigate the intentions and attitudes that lay behind them.

ACTIVITY

Re-read page 8–11s and list the reasons offered for the failure to establish Home Rule in 1914. Do these reasons offer a sufficient explanation? Do they raise any further questions? Make a list of the questions that you would like to ask, and then the sources 1 and 2 on pages 26 – 27 to develop a better explanation of why the Liberals failed to establish Home Rule in 1914. In particular, you can consider the actions of those who opposed Home Rule and the intentions behind them, as well as their underlying attitudes and ideas, in order to develop the explanation.

THINK LIKE AN HISTORIAN

The explanation in Chapter 1 was a causal explanation of the event of Irish Partition, so it focused on defining causal factors and explaining their links to the outcome. The factors were considered in relation to their effects on the issue of Partition, but some may need further explanation.

You now have a much better appreciation of how events, actions and ideas interact and the different modes of explanation that need to be used to explain them. For example, the roles of the Conservatives and Ulster Unionists were clearly important in preventing Home Rule, but historians also ask why they acted in this way. Bear in mind that the Leader of the Opposition in Britain was prepared to support violent resistance to laws passed by the elected government – what were his intentions and how did he justify this action? The Ulster Unionists were prepared to rebel against the very state to which they professed loyalty. What beliefs explain this? These questions illustrate the key point that any mode of explanation will raise issues that require the use of other modes.

Source ① Attitudes and beliefs

It might at first sight seem misleading to treat Ireland as part of the British Empire rather than the United Kingdom, but there are good reasons for doing so. During most of its unhappy history the relationship between Britain and Ireland was a colonial one. British settlers effectively colonised Ireland in the sixteenth and seventeenth centuries, as they did parts of the New World. The Irish Parliament before the Union of 1801 was treated as a colonial assembly. Thereafter despite the presence of 100 Irish MPs and 16 peers at Westminster, Ireland was still ruled by a Viceroy based in Dublin Castle and a Chief Secretary with a seat in the British Cabinet. Britain provided an imperial police force in the shape of the Royal Irish Constabulary and when trouble threatened, as it did in 1916 and again between 1919 and 1921, an occupying army was sent to maintain imperial authority.

On the credit side, the more enlightened British politicians accepted the obligations that went with imperial responsibilities. Beginning with the Land Commission set up in 1881, several British governments embarked on a range of policies designed to improve living conditions for the Irish peasantry, whereas they ignored the plight of the English agricultural labourer. A final proof that Ireland is best thought of as an imperial possession is to be found in the arguments that arose over Home Rule. The

Conservatives opposed Home Rule for Ireland, at least in part, because they feared it would be the prelude to the dismemberment of the Empire. Conversely, there was a persistent strand of anti-imperialism in Irish nationalism. Irish nationalists frequently expressed their sympathy for the other oppressed peoples of the Empire. Two volunteer Irish brigades even fought on the Boer side in the Second Boer War of 1899–1902.

But if the South sought liberation, the North East of Ireland was peculiarly linked to the United Kingdom. In Ulster, two-thirds of the population were the Protestant descendants of those Scots and English who had settled there in the seventeenth century. The seventeenth-century fight against Catholicism had been preserved through the years of a Protestant ascendancy and the reduction of the Irish to the status of landless peasants through the Penal Laws. Fear of a government elected by a Catholic majority combined with economic interests, especially in industrial Belfast, to strengthen reliance on the British connection, and as the prospect of Home Rule approached so their commitment to the British connection grew stronger.

Adapted from W. O. Simpson (1986)
Changing Horizons: Britain 1914–80,
Stanley Thornes.

Source ② Actions and reactions

Although the Home Rule Act of 1912 had been delayed by the House of Lords, it was due to become law under the terms of the Parliament Act of 1911 in the summer of 1914. In order to prevent this outcome the Ulster Volunteers, a paramilitary organisation, was formed under the active patronage of the Conservative party. Bonar Law, Leader of the Opposition, even stated that he could imagine 'no length of resistance to which Ulster can go in which I should not be ready to support them ...' As good as his word, Bonar Law was in close touch with Field Marshal Earl Roberts and Sir Henry Wilson, Director of Military Operations. He secured their approval for a plan to amend the Annual Army Act in the House of Lords in such a way that the use of the army in Ulster would have been prevented until given approval after a General Election.

The plan was rendered unnecessary by the so-called 'Curragh Mutiny'. This episode occurred in March 1914, though it was more like a strike than a mutiny. The Commander-in-Chief in Ireland, Sir Arthur Paget, fearing that those of his fellow officers who lived in Ulster might reasonably object to acting against the Ulster Volunteers, won a highly damaging concession from the War Office. Any officer domiciled in Ulster was to be allowed to 'disappear' for the period of operations, to be reinstated without penalty when they were over. Any other officer who for conscientious reasons was not prepared to carry out his duty as ordered might choose to be dismissed. Brigadier Gough and 57 out of 70 officers in the 3rd Cavalry Brigade decided to choose dismissal rather than undertake operations in Ulster. The Government took fright and persuaded Gough and the others to withdraw their threat of resignation, but only after giving an assurance that the Government would not use their right to 'crush political opposition to the policy or the principles of the Home Rule Bill'.

Clearly, the army could no longer be relied on to support the Government's own policies. Worse was to follow. In April 1914, the Ulster Volunteers succeeded in smuggling into Ireland 20,000 rifles and 3 million rounds of ammunition. In the South a comparable organisation, the Irish Volunteers, was set up to meet the threat from the North. Their efforts at gunrunning were less successful. A convoy of vehicles was intercepted at Howth in July 1914 and three lives were lost when British troops fired on a hostile but unarmed mob. The nationalists could not help but believe that while resistance in Ulster was condoned, their attempts to match it were treated as rebellion.

Adapted from W. O. Simpson (1986)
Changing Horizons: Britain 1914–80,
Stanley Thornes.

1. What different ideas existed about the relationship between England and Ireland?

2. How do these ideas help to explain
   (a) division within Ireland,
   (b) Conservative opposition to home rule.

3. What did the Conservative leaders want to achieve in their negotiations with the army?

4. What were the intentions of the army in the Curragh Mutiny?

5. What actions did the army take to deal with gunrunning in Ulster?

6. How do the attitudes described in source 1 help to explain the actions and the intentions shown in source 2?

Source 4 Martin Luther (continued)

The Catholic doctrine of purgatory

A sin is committing an offence against God. In Catholic doctrine sins could only be forgiven after repentance, confession to a priest and the carrying out of a penance. Every Catholic wanted to be prepared for death, to have repented of all their sins before dying. Repentance was of great importance, especially because sudden death was a major concern for the people of late medieval Europe (not surprising, given the regular outbreaks of war, plague and famine). Since very few would die in a fully prepared state almost everybody would have to go to purgatory, a place of waiting while souls were punished and sins were cleansed before the soul could enter heaven. Catholics believed that to enter purgatory would result in considerable suffering for the individual. This issue had become a preoccupation for late medieval people, and they had a number of strategies for dealing with it. It is significant that many of these could be carried out by the Church or by relatives on someone's behalf, both during their lifetime and after they were dead.

Prayers and masses for the dead were said in order to release loved ones from purgatory more quickly. One's own time in purgatory might be reduced through the purchase of an indulgence. Indulgences were pieces of parchment issued by the Church. Most were very specific, but some, signed by the pope, offered a general pardon for sin and therefore immediate release from purgatory. One can see why indulgences were a highly attractive proposition, but for Luther such a theology of forgiveness was problematic. In 1517 Tetzel's approach was particularly offensive to him, because Indulgences were being directly sold as a convenient way of absolving one's sins and reconciling oneself with God. Tetzel preached that 'all the ministries of Christ's passion' were embodied in these indulgences, and that they offered general pardon and instant release for souls in purgatory.

Adapted from A. Armstrong (2002) *The European Reformation*, Heinemann.

Source 5 The Church in the early sixteenth century

The role and power of the Church

For the people of late medieval Europe, religion was of great importance. The Church played a central role in their lives, not just spiritually but also socially and economically. There were few non-believers in the practices and teachings of Catholicism. People generally believed that the Church provided all the right answers and that it was only through the Catholic Church that salvation could be attained. In general, religious activity was about participating as part of the community. The Church was central to life in towns and villages alike through all sorts of activities. Religious processions and pilgrimages to local shrines were popular, while feast days and saints' days attracted large crowds and were observed universally by the people. The church was a most important social centre for the people – a natural gathering point in what was predominantly a rural society.

Most people believed in the power and importance of religious relics. Scepticism did not exist, and relics such as thorns from the crown of Christ or splinters from the True Cross were similarly bought or worshipped. The most famous relics were centres of major pilgrimage, and brought in a good income for the churches where they were kept. There was a widespread belief that miracles were performed at the shrines of saints, and most people adopted a saint who they believed looked after them through curing illness or protecting crops. The most popular image was that of Our Lady, Mary, mother of Jesus. Throughout Europe, people paid for her image to beam down from windows or to inspire through statues.

What does source 4 suggest about the nature of Luther's ideas and their implications?

How serious were his differences with the Church over matters of doctrine?

Source (5) **The Church in the early sixteenth century (continued)**

All this brought the Church a significant income, much of it given voluntarily. Churchwardens' accounts from across Europe reveal the amount of money contributed by a community towards the upkeep, maintenance and expansion of churches during this period. Ornately gilded churches, glitteringly adorned with figures of saints, were in some ways testament to the devotion of the people. Large amounts of money were left in wills to the Church and the laity also regularly paid taxation to the Church, often in the form of the tithe, which amounted to a tenth of all income and produce. Moreover, mortuary dues (money paid when people died), the Peter's Pence (a tax payable to the papacy) and the buying of indulgences represent other economic links between the laity and the Church. The taxes were regularly paid with little resentment, but payments were not always popular. There is evidence of anti-clerical feeling caused by the extent of taxation, especially in Germany where the lack of a strong central government allowed the Church to make heavy demands.

The problems facing the Church

The nature of religious belief and practice shows that there could often be a fine line between belief and superstition, and that many of the customs allowed superstition to be exploited. By the early sixteenth century the Church was facing a number of problems, centred on accusations of corruption and spiritual weakness.

The Papacy

The pope in Rome hardly set a good example. In 1500 the papacy was a powerful institution politically and spiritually, but it was also going through a particularly bad period. The pope was generally Italian and, although technically an elected position, through bribery it had become dominated by aristocratic Italian families such as the Medicis. Popes were political figures, ruling their own state in Italy and exercising great international influence. Top of most historians' lists of badly behaved popes comes Alexander VI (1431–1503). Formerly Rodrigo Borgia, Alexander VI was made a cardinal by his uncle, Pope Calixtus III, in 1455 before becoming pope himself in 1492 on the death of Innocent VIII. It was widely recognised that Alexander owed his position to the widespread bribery of the College of Cardinals. Although Alexander started brightly by restoring order in Rome and challenging the authority of the Italian princes, he soon held a string of mistresses and fathered a number of illegitimate children, most of whom were looked after with clerical titles and income. In total, Alexander appointed 47 cardinals, including his teenage son Cesare. The luxury of the Alexandrian papal court knew no bounds while, as a patron of the arts, Alexander grew in stature, even commissioning Michelangelo to draw up plans for the rebuilding of St Peter's Basilica in Rome. Political manoeuvring and the furthering of his family were more important to Alexander than spiritual matters. However, papal authority was defended – in 1498, he did oversee the burning of Girolamo Savonarola, an influential friar from Florence, who had been convicted of denying papal authority and preaching heretical doctrine. In 1503, Alexander died when he accidentally took poison at a dinner party hosted by Cardinal de Corneto. The poison had been intended for the host! Julius II (1503–13), the Warrior Pope, cared more about preserving Papal power in Europe amid aggression from France and the Holy Roman Empire, while the next Pope, Leo X (1513–21) was obsessed with the building of the grandest church in Christendom, St Peter's Basilica in Rome.

THINK LIKE AN HISTORIAN

Before you begin, re-read the empathetic explanation of Marxism and Marxist-Leninism on page 21–22. Keep these ideas in mind as you work through the task, to see how they influenced both expectations and actions leading to the Revolution. One way to approach this is by asking whether (a) the revolution would have taken place without Lenin, and (b) whether Lenin's actions would have been the same without his belief in the Marxist dialectic.

Your explanation will therefore begin by considering the role of ideas, develop through using other modes of explanation, and then return to ideas to explain their role in a more specific way.

Case study 3: The Bolshevik Revolution in Russia, 1917

It is therefore logical to begin any explanation of the Bolshevik Revolution by exploring these underlying ideas. However, that does not adequately explain why there was a Bolshevik Revolution in Russia in 1917. Understanding of the Bolsheviks' ideas explains their aims, and to some extent their motives but cannot explain why they were able to take power at that particular time. To develop the explanation further, it is necessary to consider the events that created the opportunity and the actions that they took in response. Source 6 will enable you to do this.

ACTIVITY

Re-read the empathetic explanation on page 21–22 (Chapter 1) and summarise the ways in which Marxist and Leninist ideas encouraged those who sought change in Russia to work for a revolution. Then read source 6 and answer the following questions:

1. Which events created the opportunity for the Bolsheviks to seize power in October 1917?

2. In what ways did the actions of individuals contribute to the eventual outcome?

3. How important were ideas in shaping the events of October 1917?

Source 6 — Lenin and the Russian Revolution

At the beginning of 1917 the Romanov dynasty, which had governed Russia for just over three hundred years, was in a perilous state. The Tsarist regime of Nicholas II was under severe pressure from many sides. Even before the outbreak of the First World War, the Tsar's government had found it difficult to cope with the strains caused by industrialisation and the increasing demands for political change. The Tsarist system of government was considered by many educated Russians to be outdated. However, the limited size of the bourgeoisie in Russia made liberal reforms unlikely, and many of the intellectuals had already adopted Marxist ideas of revolution as the only way to move forward. The regime had survived an attempted revolution in 1905 but only by making concessions under severe duress. In order to isolate and destroy the socialists and workers of the St Petersburg Soviet, the Tsar promised constitutional reform to win the support of the liberals.

These had included the establishment of a parliament, the Duma, but as soon as it began to demand radical change the Tsar issued Fundamental Laws that restricted the right to vote and deprived the Duma of real power. Industrialisation continued, and so did unrest. Attempts were made at land reform, to ease the condition of the peasants, but these had made little real progress before the outbreak of war in 1914.

When war broke out in 1914 the stresses and strains already present in Russia were greatly exacerbated by the sheer scale and duration of the First World War. Although Russia still had a vast peasant army, the weakness of transport and industrial systems meant that they went into battle with inadequate weapons and ammunition. By 1916 the Germans had advanced far into Russia and Russian losses were enormous. As one general remarked, 'The Germans expend metal where we expend blood.' At home there were food shortages and a flood of refugees that simply could not be cared for. In 1916 Nicholas went to the front to take personal control of the war – an error that made him personally responsible for further defeats. It also left government in the hands of his unpopular German wife. By February 1917 government in Russia was in chaos and, under pressure from both opposition groups and his own supporters, Tsar Nicholas II abdicated. The country then fell into the hands of a Provisional Government.

Source 6 — Lenin and the Russian Revolution (continued)

Formed from the Duma, the new government was a weak and unstable grouping of politicians trying desperately to gain some control over events. Led initially by Prince Lvov and after July 1917 by Kerensky, the Provisional Government faced the same problems as the Tsar and was unable to offer any effective solutions. From the start it lacked both authority and support. The Duma had been elected on a restricted franchise, and the Provisional Government had to rely on co-operation from the Petrograd Soviet, which represented the workers (and later soldiers and some peasants). This was not always whole-hearted. However, the Provisional Government rapidly made things worse by a decision to continue with the war.

The war was at the root of many problems, and as long as it continued there was no real prospect of meaningful reform. The government abolished titles and established some political freedom, but it could not provide adequate food supplies, restore the collapsing infrastructure or stem the flow of blood and defeat on the battlefields. To make matters worse the decision was taken to delay calling a Constituent Assembly and hold back on land reform until the war was over. They allowed the peasants to seize land from the Tsar and the Church, thereby encouraging desertions from the army as peasant soldiers sought to get home and take their share. By July the government appeared to be on the verge of collapse, after a major new offensive produced another military disaster and the Germans were advancing on Petrograd. A workers' revolt led by some of the Bolsheviks was crushed, but within weeks there was a new threat as the Tsarist general, Kornilov, announced his intention of taking control to restore order in Petrograd. The political authority of the government was ebbing away.

Meanwhile the Bolsheviks had been gaining some support. They had played no distinct role in the revolution of February, simply encouraging popular action alongside other socialists, and helping them to establish the Petrograd Soviet, where they were very much in the minority. Most socialists in Russia accepted the need to support the bourgeois revolution that had taken place in February and allow Russia to go through its stage of capitalist development in order to advance towards socialism. In April, however, Lenin had returned from exile in Switzerland, and immediately set about organising a distinctive Bolshevik campaign. Issuing his April Theses, he had argued that the extent of Russia's collapse would allow the Bolsheviks to seize power and move straight to a socialist regime. He determined that the Bolsheviks would challenge the Provisional Government at every opportunity, and build up support among the workers, peasants and soldiers by demanding an end to the war. Using the slogan of 'Peace, bread, land', they sought to channel popular discontent into Bolshevik support and to blame the leaders of the Soviet for supporting the government. The abortive revolt of July was a disaster, driving Lenin back into exile in nearby Finland, but he continued to direct the campaign and to return secretly as needed. Other leading Bolsheviks such as Kamenev and Trotsky were arrested, but released with others in August to join in resistance to Kornilov. By September Bolshevik support was rising again, and they gained a small majority within the Petrograd Soviet, with Trotsky as its President.

By late September Lenin was convinced that the time was right to stage an armed attempt for power. Other Bolsheviks, including Kamenev and Zinoniev, were opposed to such an idea, arguing that a rising would leave the party isolated. But for Lenin the time was right and delay could lead to a downturn in their fortunes. Although he had the support of Trotsky, it was Lenin's determination that won the day, and it is here that his importance is seen. He had the ability to persuade his party of the necessity for immediate revolution; a revolution that could be undertaken with the support of the Soviet and the Red Guards. He also had the help of a brilliant tactician in Leon Trotsky, whose role within the Soviet allowed him to organise military action by the Red Guards and their allies. For Lenin this was the

> ### Source ⑥ Lenin and the Russian Revolution (continued)
>
> culmination of a lifetime's devotion to an idea – the Marxist dialectic – and a belief that it could be adapted, as he had argued since 1903, to conditions in Russia.
>
> What decided the timing of the revolution was action by Kerensky. Aware that the Bolsheviks posed a threat, he decided to close down their newspapers and arrest key leaders. However, he was too slow. Lenin and Trotsky evaded arrest and implemented their plans to seize power. Here the advantage of Lenin's insistence on a small, elite organisation helped the Bolsheviks – their members were loyal and secrecy was maintained. The key positions in Petrograd were seized by Red Guards under the direction of the Military Revolution Committee of the Soviet, co-ordinated by Trotsky. Power stations, police stations, bridges and the rail network in Petrograd were all in Bolshevik hands when the sailors of the battleship Aurora pointed its guns at the Winter Palace and fired a single shot as a signal for action. This intimidated the Provisional Government into surrendering what little power it had.
>
> Adapted from S. Philips (2000)
> *Lenin and the Russian Revolution,*
> Heinemann.

How modes of explanation are interlinked

Case studies 1–3 demonstrated how different modes of explanation interact, because ideas, actions and events interact to bring about particular outcomes. Whatever mode is initially used, a sufficient explanation is unlikely to be established without using the other two modes, because the nature of historical explanation is to raise new questions as the explanation is developed. This is because the initial mode adopted is dictated by the question that is asked. If the historian begins with a question such as 'Why was there a Bolshevik Revolution in Russia in 1917?', they are focusing on an event which will require the use of the causal mode. If, however, the question is 'Why did the Bolsheviks seize power in Russia in 1917?', the event is being seen as an action, and will require a focus on the actions, motives and intentions of the Bolsheviks, especially their leaders. Whichever mode is adopted first, the Bolshevik Revolution cannot be adequately explained without considering the events and situations that made it possible (*causal*), the actions that brought success (*intentional*) and the ideas that guided these actions (*empathetic*). Hence all three modes are required.

This process of building up an explanation by interlinking different modes can be explained and illustrated in further case studies. To establish the stages within the process we can consider an outline example. On Christmas day 800 CE, the Frankish ruler Charlemagne was crowned as as emperor by the Pope, Leo III, in Rome in a symbolic revival of the western Roman Empire, which had collapsed under barbarian invasions in the fifth and sixth centuries. This event marked the height of Frankish power and the confirmation of an empire that stretched from the Pyrenees to the Baltic and down the valley of the Danube. It also defined the division of the old Roman Empire into eastern and western halves, with momentous consequences for European development. To show *why* this happened we can adopt a causal explanation, but to understand its significance and *explain what happened* we need to go further and consider *why Charlemagne chose to take this action, and what it meant for him and his subjects.* For this, we need to use both the intentional and empathetic modes of explanation.

We can begin by defining a key question and some sub-questions that arise from it. The question: 'Why was Charlemagne crowned as emperor in Rome in 800 CE?' can be broken down into these sub-questions:

- Why was it possible for the event to take place?

- Why did it happen at that time?

- Why did Charlemagne choose to take this title?

- What did the title signify or symbolise?

To answer the first part, we can consider three factors: Charlemagne's inheritance of a strong Frankish kingdom from his father, Pepin the Short; his own success as ruler of the Franks in conquering Lombard Italy, Bavaria, Saxony and the Danubian Avars; and his alliance with the Church. These three factors created the conditions in which Charlemagne's coronation could be arranged and managed, and are therefore *conditional factors*. The event was triggered by quarrels within the Church in 799, which led Pope Leo to flee from Rome to Charlemagne's court for protection. Frankish troops restored him to Rome. This was the *contingent factor* that influenced the timing of the event.

However, this *causal* explanation of the event does not explain why Charlemagne wanted to do this. To address this issue we need to consider the event as an *action* and explain his *motives and intentions* – but that cannot be done without understanding the significance of the title and the *attitudes and beliefs* to which it was linked. The Roman Empire represented a golden age of peace and security, to which medieval rulers and their subjects looked back with respect and longing. It also represented Christianity as against the paganism of northern Europe. It was the significance of Christianity as the religion of the later empire that allowed the popes in Rome to claim both temporal and spiritual power as the heirs of the emperors, challenging the claims made by the eastern, Byzantine emperors to authority over the west. Therefore, by accepting the title of emperor Charlemagne was seen by some as the status of a Roman emperor and a leader of Christianity, as well as setting limits to Byzantine power. This *empathetic* explanation now allows us to understand his action – his *intentions* were to consolidate his own power and define the role of his allies in the Church.

EXAM TIP

When faced with a question, it is always important to analyse it carefully in order to define the focus. The key to exam success is always to ensure that you answer the question rather than simply writing about the topic. Therefore, you need to consider its main focus, and formulate an appropriate starting point, but to develop a full response you can also consider a range of sub-questions to explore the issues more fully. You can use the labels of *event*, *actions* and *ideas*, and the appropriate modes of explanation, as is demonstrated here.

Although this explanation is brief and necessarily simplified, it does illustrate the process involved in building historical explanations, and clarifies the role of different factors so that their interlinking can be analysed. This not only develops the explanation in itself, but enables other issues, such as the relative importance of different factors to be considered. We can therefore summarise a number of stages, as shown in Figure 2.1.

1. Begin with **what needs to be explained** – an event or situation, an action or an 'idea'. Define it in these terms and **set out a question** that is appropriate to both the occurrence and the required mode of explanation. Note: in exam situations, this will have been done for you.

2. Plan your explanation in outline (as with the Charlemagne question) according to the appropriate mode. As you do this, look for other **sub-questions** that can develop the explanation, such as (a) what conditions made it possible, (b) what actions contributed to it, and (c) what beliefs and attitudes encouraged or influenced the outcome? The sub-questions can set the shape and order of your arguments, and highlight the **role of different factors** within the overall explanation. They will also invoke other modes of explanation as appropriate.

3. Work through the sub-questions to build your explanation, and summarise your conclusions with explicit reference to the role of different factors within an overall explanation.

   This will include explanation of how they **interlinked**.

❚ **Figure 2.1** The process of building historical explanations

This process is illustrated in the final case study below – an essay written as a response to an exam question: 'Why did revolution break out in France in 1789?'. It is a good example of how a key question can be broken down into sub-questions, in which one mode of explanation invokes another.

ACTIVITY

To see this for yourself, as you read the essay, highlight sections in different colours to identify which mode is being used, and how the essay moves from one to another. It would also be useful to underline statements in each section that make explicit causal links to the revolution, or to the role of a particular factor in contributing to its outbreak. The same applies to statements in the conclusion that explain how factors interlinked.

To enable you to make best use of this exercise, a copy of the essay is included on the CD ROM so that you can print, edit and keep it for future reference.

EXAM TIP

As you read the essay, notice the style in which it is written. It is different from the way in which an historian might write in a textbook. The purpose of a textbook is to explain to readers, who may well have little prior knowledge of the topic, what happened. The historian's role is to inform the reader and this may well necessitate substantial passages of narrative or description alongside the explanations offered. An essay is intended as a response to a particular question, which requires analysis and the construction of arguments. For that purpose the approach should be analytical, as it is in the example in case study 4, and 'information' is included to support different arguments and demonstrate their accuracy. Information should not be included for its own sake, but only if it is directly relevant to the task in hand – which is answering the actual question set.

Case study 4: Why did revolution break out in France in 1789?

THINK LIKE AN HISTORIAN

Before you begin to read the essay, you might find it useful to analyse the question as an historian would, and as we did in the case of Charlemagne. This is a big question, about a complex event.

Historians might well want to define it more carefully, for example by considering whether it is about 'a' revolution or 'the' revolution that broke out in 1789. If it is 'a' revolution, the focus of the arguments will be on the general causes that made a revolution likely at some time. If it is 'the' revolution, then there is a need to look at what made it happen then. Factors such as individual actions and mistakes may well be more important. What sub-questions would you ask to make this question more manageable and help to organise your response?

The revolution of 1789 was a complex event, developing in stages across the summer of 1789. The Estates-General had been summoned to consider reforms that would have modified the existing system of government in order to make it work more effectively. Instead it brought about the collapse of absolutism, the establishment of a representative assembly, and the direct intervention of the 'people' through events such as the fall of the Bastille, the Great Fear and the October days. By the autumn of 1789, when the king was forcibly brought back to Paris by direct, deliberate, popular action (unlike the fall of the Bastille and the Great Fear, which were both popular reactions to rumours and fears) it was clear that royal power had effectively collapsed. To explain these events it is necessary to consider what had led up to the situation, and why it had developed in this way, by addressing a range of conditional and contingent factors.

It had been clear for some years that the social and political structure of France was in need of reform. The king ruled as an absolute monarch, his power justified by Divine Right and based on the support of the nobility and Church. They controlled land, exercised law and justice in their own estates, and helped to enforce royal decrees. A centralised bureaucracy based on an administrative nobility as well as bourgeois office-holders carried out royal government on the direct authority of the king. In return, these privileged orders were exempt from most taxation, leaving the 'third estate' of peasants, townsmen and tradesmen to bear most of the expenses of government. While some were wealthy bourgeoisie, the great majority were peasants struggling under a burden of feudal dues to their landlords as well as royal taxation. Not only was this unjust, it was also inefficient. Taxation was collected by tax 'farmers' who estimated revenue, paid the government a fixed sum and then collected the money at a profit. Both the structure and administration of government ensured that the monarchy was only able to access a limited part of the country's resources, while the people struggled under crushing economic burdens.

This was compounded by an expensive foreign policy and a concern for prestige, which had led to a series of wars against other powers, especially Britain. Britain and France were rivals for empire in both North America and India, but France was also a continental power, forced to defend land boundaries and seeking expansion in Europe. The Seven Years War of 1756–63 saw France lose her possessions in North America and suffer defeat in Europe with her Austrian ally at the hands of Prussia. The combination of failure and vast expense undermined the prestige of the monarchy. In 1778–83 France gained revenge by supporting the American

EXAM TIP

This is a useful introduction, which attempts to define the issues posed by the question. The question is relatively open, addressing 'revolution' rather than defining what precisely the revolution consisted of, and the introduction helps to define the focus and make the question more manageable. The candidate is able to take control of the response and direct it. The reference to events and to conditional and contingent factors identifies a causal mode of explanation, and also gives shape to what is to come by defining key sub-questions – what led up to the situation and how it developed.

colonists against Britain, but this only led to further expense for no direct gain. While the monarch maintained a luxurious lifestyle and the unpopular Austrian queen Marie-Antoinette was nicknamed 'Madam Deficit' for her extravagance, the government was increasingly able to function only by taking out huge loans, so that by the early 1780s the payment of interest was taking up a good part of royal revenue. This was disguised by the Compte Rendu [statement of accounts issued by Necker in 1781] which ignored expenditure on war, but by 1786 the Controller General of Finance, Calonne, estimated that government was running on an annual deficit of 100 million livres.

By 1786 this combination of failure, inefficiency and injustice was causing serious discontent among all sections of French society, at a time when attitudes and beliefs were changing in a way that threatened the basis of the monarchy. The eighteenth century had seen the development of an 'enlightenment' across Europe, which was derived from the development of scientific knowledge and emphasised the need for all aspects of life to be governed by reason and rational processes. Scientists like Newton had shown that the universe operated according to natural laws, while writers like Montesquieu and Rousseau applied the same concepts to social and political relationships. As these ideas gained popularity, the contrast with the chaotic and unfair basis of government in France became increasingly apparent, and encouraged a demand for reform from within the privileged orders as well as from the educated bourgeoisie. What was particularly serious for the king was the impact of such ideas on religious belief, which was the basis of his power. The beliefs that underpinned divine right monarchy were increasingly dismissed as superstition. Without divine right, the king had no right, and the needs of the people should be the guiding principle of government.

It was these changing attitudes that helped to bring the crisis to a head. Louis XVI was a well-intentioned monarch, who accepted the need for reform but proved unable to control events and see it through in the face of opposition. This was partly a matter of his indecisive character. He appointed two able financial advisers in Turgot and Necker, but then allowed them to be driven from office by Court intrigues, encouraged by the queen. He then appointed Calonne in 1783, but refused to support his ideas for reform or cut back on personal expenditure until bankruptcy threatened in 1786. When Calonne met resistance from the privileged orders in 1787, the king replaced him with Brienne. When Brienne faced a clash with the Paris Parlement the king exiled the Parlement to Troyes, then withdrew the decision in the face of popular demonstrations. However, the king's inconsistent behaviour was also a response to public and private pressure, created by changes in the fundamental political attitudes and beliefs held in French society.

The core of resistance to reform came from the privileged orders, on whose co-operation the monarchy depended. Led first by the Assembly of Notables and then by the Parlements, the nobility and sections of the Church refused to accept the proposals put forward by ministers unless they were accompanied by political changes and the sharing of power. The cry of 'ministerial despotism' was raised to gain public support, but it also reflected a fundamental loss of confidence in both the king and the system of absolute monarchy, caused by its failure, inefficiency and injustice. Although personal rivalries and selfish interests contributed to the situation, the ability of the notables to appeal to public opinion rested, not on resistance to reform, but on insistence that a more significant review and reform was necessary. The limited schemes of reform that Louis and his ministers could envisage were insufficient to satisfy a society influenced by enlightenment ideas, and failed. In 1788 the impending bankruptcy became unavoidable, the king restored the popular Necker to power, and agreed to summon the Estates-General for the first time since 1714. Although occasioned by financial collapse, the situation reflected the bankruptcy of absolute monarchy and divine right on a far wider scale. It is clear, therefore, that the conditions that allowed revolution to occur in France in 1789 arose from a combination of factors — the underlying weakness of the system, the financial problems caused by war and extravagance, the changing climate of ideas and beliefs, and the mistakes made by individuals, especially the king. However, these factors are not sufficient to explain the outbreak of revolution. When the Estates-General met in May 1789 the agenda was still focused on reform, and the role of the monarch was still seen as central to the process. What triggered the outbreak of revolution was a series of mistakes made by the king, which reflected his lack of political understanding and the extent to which his attitudes were still rooted in concepts of divine right. Although he agreed to the Third Estate having double the representation of the First and Second orders, he then destroyed its effects by insisting on voting by estate, which meant that the privileged orders could still outvote the representatives of the people. The reforms proposed by the king and Necker on 5 May were completely inadequate, and Louis' reaction to the establishment of the National Assembly was utterly negative, despite the actions of some of the privileged orders in supporting it. The closing of the hall, which triggered the Tennis Court Oath, was accidental and unintended in its effects, but the willingness of deputies to believe that it was a deliberate slight was a result of the attitudes that the king had conveyed. Similarly, the gathering troops in Paris that triggered the fall of the Bastille, and the banquet with the Flanders regiment that provoked the October days reflected the king's underlying attitudes and desire to resist change as far as possible. It can therefore be suggested that what caused revolution in France in 1789 was the behaviour of a monarch who was unable to recognise the impact of events and the climate of ideas that made fundamental change unavoidable.

This is a coherent and reasonably comprehensive explanation of the outbreak of revolution, drawing on a range of factors and appropriate modes of explanation. The overall structure treats 'revolution' as an event, and adopts a causal approach using both conditional and contingent factors. However, where these factors involve ideas and actions, the essay uses an empathetic or intentional mode to explain the nature and role of that factor effectively. Links are established between the various factors to show how the situation built up towards the eventual outcome.

The importance of critical evaluation

The essay above is focused primarily on building an explanation and does so very effectively. However, the best explanations can go even further by critically evaluating the explanation that has been offered. In this essay, the role of different factors is outlined but not fully explored. To achieve this, an explanation needs to be subjected to a critical analysis that breaks it down into its component parts, evaluates the role of different factors to establish relative importance and synthesises them into an integrated explanation. To do this requires a process of review that can only be carried out once the explanation is broadly established.

For example, if we return to Mr Brown's car crash, we have already analysed the events into causal factors – his attitude to work, the effects on his marriage and his neglect of his car are the conditional factors that made an accident likely, while the events of that particular night (being late/driving fast, the rain and the dog on the road) are the contingencies that defined the nature and timing of the crash. We have therefore defined their role, the links between them and the part that they played in the crash. We can use certain techniques to assess which were the most important factors.

One way to analyse the role of these factors more fully and to assess which were the more important is to ask: 'Which factors were necessary to offer a *sufficient explanation* of the crash?'

To answer this, we can consider whether the outcome would have been the same if any factors were not present. If we reduce the number of factors to those that were essential to cause the crash, we may be able to argue that they were the most important factors, while others played a lesser part in the outcome. For example, it could be said that the crash would not have happened without the dog on the road, because that caused Mr Brown to brake and skid. The worn tyre and the rain may well have contributed to this, but it is possible that an accident would still have occurred without these factors, particularly as Mr Brown was driving fast. His speed was caused by being late, and his anxiety to keep his promise, so these factors were also essential – without these pressures he could have been driving more cautiously and been able to brake safely. It can therefore be argued that Mr Brown's working habits made a crash of some kind likely, and the dog triggered it – these two factors alone offer a sufficient explanation of the crash, although the other factors still help to explain its nature and severity.

An alternative approach would be to ask: 'Were any factors caused by, or *dependent on* other factors?' If so, it would be logical to conclude that the factors giving rise to other factors were the most important. For example, the situation in which Mr Brown was driving home fast was caused by his habit of working long hours and the effect that it had on his wife. The fact that his car had not been properly maintained also arose from his working habits. It could therefore be argued that this underlying problem was the most important factor, causing the situation. However, the rain and the dog were separate causes, not related to Mr Brown or his actions. Therefore, his crash can be explained by the interaction of his working habits and the random factors of the rain and the dog.

The two approaches have produced a similar, but not identical conclusion. This is because they are not based on 'facts' but on inference and deduction, as the basis of a developed judgement. The key point is not that these arguments can achieve certainty – they are based on judgement – but that they lead us into analysing the role of different factors more fully. We can therefore attribute relative significance or importance to different factors, thereby drawing conclusions about their overall *interaction* and *synthesising* them into a developed and integrated explanation. To explore this more fully, you can apply the two techniques to analysing the essay above.

THINK LIKE AN HISTORIAN

'Review' literally means to look again at ideas and arguments that have been built up and supported. Historians are aware that their arguments and explanations involve judgement, which needs to be substantiated and explained fully.

Historians often work by a process of hypothesis-testing, as outlined in chapter 1, page 3, in which evidence and knowledge of what happened is used to suggest an idea (or explanation) that is then tested and developed further by looking at more evidence. What historians do in critically evaluating their own work is to subject it to a similar process, by asking further questions and trying to re-examine their judgements.

In an essay this can take the form of a developed conclusion in which you re-examine the key points in the explanation using the role of factors and their interaction to establish another level of judgement: which factors were the most important?

ACTIVITY

Re-read the explanation of why revolution broke out in France in 1789 and use each approach in turn to analyse the role, significance and interaction of the different factors involved. You can use the list of factors set out in the final paragraph, or if you prefer, you can begin by redefining them for yourself. The key is then to analyse the arguments critically, looking to explore the role of each factor, demonstrate its links with the other factors, and assess the relative significance that can be attributed to each one. Then write a summary conclusion explaining the interaction and relative importance of different factors in causing revolution in France in 1789.

Summary

Chapter 1 introduced you to the existence and nature of different modes of explanation in the study of history, and the techniques that are appropriate for explaining different types of 'fact' as part of what happened. Chapter 2 has focused on the process by which one mode of explanation raises issues and questions that invoke other modes, on how these can be combined and integrated to offer better explanations and how they can be used to develop judgements about what happened and why. We can now summarise the whole process of historical explanation.

- It begins with 'what happened' according to evidence found in historical sources – both left by contemporaries and developed later by historians.

- Historians analyse 'what happened' to define key questions about causes, effects and significance. In exam situations this is done for you, and you must answer the question that is asked – but you can do this on different levels and build better answers by recognising the new questions and sub-questions that they create.

- Questions focus on different types of 'fact' – events and situations, actions and the role of individuals, and the attitudes and values that influence them. To create an explanation, first *define the nature of what is to be explained,* and then *apply the appropriate mode of explanation.*

- Be aware that explanations will always include different types of factors, and that if *any one mode is adequately developed, it will raise new questions that invoke others.* The nature of these new questions depends on you – there is no single 'right' format. It is up to you to explore the issues and form your own explanations. Explanations offered by historians can give you ideas, create a guide and encourage you to ask particular questions.

- Your explanations should include *evidence to support* the existence of different factors, the *role that they played* and the links between them, and the ways in which they *combined and interlinked* (or interacted) to bring about the outcome that you are trying to explain.

- When you have built up your explanation, you can develop it further *by reviewing or re-examining* it in a process of *critical analysis and evaluation,* to explain the role and relative importance of different factors in the overall process.

If others disagree, you can defend your judgements, but always be aware that this is what they are – judgements based on the evidence of what happened as you have understood and interpreted it. As you find out more about what happened, including others' interpretations of it, you can go on developing your historical explanations.

Exam Café

Relax, refresh, result!

Tudor finale: the reign of Elizabeth, 1558–1603

Relax and prepare

Hot tips

Martin

"I downloaded past papers from the OCR website and practised either planning how to answer the questions or timing myself to write a full essay. This made me less nervous about sitting the real thing and also able to think about the different ways similar questions can be asked."

Ravinder

"My teacher made sure we understood the key issues in this topic, which really helped me to understand the sort of questions that might be asked in the exam."

Jenny

I made a revision plan for my GCSEs but didn't stick to it. For A Level I am going to make sure my plan is realistic – and I'll make sure stick to it!"

Gettingstarted...

Understanding exam questions

Each topic has terms and words that are important. Are you aware of those words that are relevant to the topic you are studing?

Check the dates that are referred to in the questions. Your historical evidence should be confined to the time period that you are being asked to write about.

Common mistakes

Chris

I think it helps if you can spell key names and events! Also, make sure you don't get similar events confused in a topic – for example, where there is more than one war, government, monarch, election, and so on.

Raj

I didn't know what the words in the exam question meant, so guessed what the question was asking. In my case, I didn't know the difference betweeen 'foreign' and 'imperial' policy. It's taught me that I need to learn the terminology – and not to guess!

Refresh your memory

Key areas of knowledge for this topic are:

▷ Catholics and Puritans: the religious settlement of 1558–59 and its aftermath.

▷ The problems posed by Mary, Queen of Scots.

▷ The struggle with Spain.

▷ The problem of men and marriage.

▷ The governance of Elizabethan England.

▷ The growth and treatment of poverty in Elizabethan England.

▷ Cultural Renaissance: Gloriana and the cult of Majesty.

Examiner's tip

Have you got thorough notes on all these aspects of the topic? Remember, it's easy to simply keep revising the parts of a topic you know and like; it's more difficult to concentrate on those bits you don't like..

Get the result!

Exam question

Why was it assumed that Elizabeth would marry?

Ravinder's answer

Elizabeth became queen in November 1558 on the death of her half sister Mary. Elizabeth was 25 years old and for the rest of her life the question of whether she should marry and whom she should marry was a serious problem.

There were a number of serious contenders to marry Elizabeth. Should it be an Englishman? The two main English contenders were Robert Dudley, Earl of Leicester and Christopher Hatton. Leicester was a very close friend of Elizabeth and was a serious contender in the earlier part of her reign. He died in 1588. Hatton was a rival of Leicester in the 1570s. Edward de Vere, Earl of Oxford was also considered a candidate. However, there were also a number of foreign princes. The most notable were, in the 1560s, Archduke Charles of Austria, who was brother of the Holy Roman Emperor, and the second one was Francis, Duke of Alençon, who was the fourth son of Henry II of France. The Duke of Alençon was the most likely candidate and Elizabeth very nearly married him in the 1570s.

However, despite these various contenders, Elizabeth never married, so why was it assumed that she would marry? In the sixteenth century society was dominated by men in all walks of life and it was expected that women should get married and have children. Therefore, it was naturally expected by everyone that the queen would marry at the earliest opportunity. However, there were other political pressures that expected marriage.

There had been very few queens who had ruled on their own and it was assumed that Elizabeth would not be able to govern without the help of a husband. Her sister, Mary I, and her cousin, Mary, Queen of Scots had both married while in the same circumstances as Elizabeth. More importantly, Elizabeth was expected to get married in order to have children and, therefore, secure the line of succession, which was needed in order to have political stability. The problem of the succession was a high priority in Tudor England.

Examiner says:

Introduction is very brief but to the point.

Examiner says:

This second paragraph is a very good example of a common fault of many candidates. It looks good on the face of it, but it only provides descriptive information about the marriage contenders.

It does not provide any explanation as to why Elizabeth should marry.

Remember, just giving facts is not sufficient to attain a good mark at AS Level.

Examiner says:

The last two paragraphs are more focused on answering the question. A line of argument is beginning to develop.

The linking sentence at the end of each of these paragraphs is a good idea.

The need for a line of succession was clearly shown in 1562 when Elizabeth nearly died of smallpox. This showed the vulnerability of life in the sixteenth century, as Elizabeth was only 29. This situation was of great concern to Elizabeth's political advisers, particularly the Privy Council, who became one of the main pressures on the queen to marry. The added concern was that until 1585 if Elizabeth died without a heir then a serious successor to the throne was her Catholic cousin, Mary, Queen of Scots, and that prospect was a very serious threat to the leading protestant supporters of Elizabeth.

The marriage of the monarch was also of concern to leading courtiers who were eager to be connected to a favourable faction at Court. This was particularly true if the marriage contenders were English aristocracy rather than foreigners. This had been clearly shown in Henry VIII's reign. The fact that in Elizabeth's reign it would be a male aristocrat who would benefit made the prize of marriage all the greater.

Foreign policy was also a consideration, which added pressure for the queen to marry. If Elizabeth married a foreign prince then the marriage settlement would have become part of a treaty or an alliance, which would have been used to further English interests abroad. There were many at Court who were concerned about the instability in European politics and England's security in a Europe that was gradually being divided along religious lines. Relations with France and Spain were of great importance and this shows the significance of the proposed marriage to Alençon in the 1570s.

Therefore, it can be seen that there were a number of reasons why it was assumed that Elizabeth would marry but the most important reason was the need to produce an heir to the throne and so secure the succession, which had been a problem for the Tudors throughout the sixteenth century.

Exam Café
Relax, refresh, result!

Russia in turmoil, 1900–24

Relax and prepare

Tom

"Our teacher suggested we check our notes carefully after each lesson. That was great advice, because sometimes my writing was illegible so I wrote out my notes again while the lesson was still fresh in my memory.

It also meant I could check I understood everything. Taking a bit of extra time and trouble paid off when I came to revise."

Hot tips
Anne-Marie

"Get a folder and get organised! The notes come thick and fast and you need to collect them together properly, because you're going to need really good notes for revision."

Getting started. . .

Are my notes ready for the exam?

▷ *Do I know the key events of the topic?*
You need to know the story of what happened in order to understand the reasons for the events. (Look in the Refresh section opposite to know what the key events are.)

▷ *Have I thought about what questions I am likely to be asked in the exam?*
Remember, this exam is concerned with REASONS, e.g. Why did the 1905 Revolution fail? Why did Tsar Nicholas take Russia into war in 1914? Why did the Provisional Government fail to survive in 1917? Why did Lenin sign the Treaty of Brest-Litovsk in March 1918?

▷ *Have I understood the theory of historical explanation?*
What are the different types of explanation that you are expected to know?
(a) causal, (b) intentional, and (c) empathetic.

REFRESH YOUR MEMORY

This topic has a number of key events and issues that must be understood. (For further detailed explanation look at the course specification for Unit F982 on the OCR website.)

▷ The 1905 Revolution.

▷ Russia, 1905–14: an enlightened despotism?

▷ 1917: The February Revolution.

▷ 1917: The Provisional Government and the October Revolution.

▷ 1917: The October Revolution.

▷ 1917–21: The Consolidation of Bolshevik Power.

You will have to answer ONE question from a choice of two, but remember that each question is divided into two parts. Each part is an essay which concentrates on a *different* aspect of historical explanation. To help you, the type of explanation required is given to you with the question, for example.

Planning Answers

▶ Read the question carefully. Candidates often glance at a question, see a particular word or phrase and assume they understand the question and start writing immediately.

▶ Plan your answer. A common, mistake is where a candidate forgets a piece of information, which is subsequently added to the essay with an asterisk. A plan could help you to avoid this. Remember, the examiner is looking for your ability to present a coherent argument.

▶ Have you ever had that moment in an exam when your mind goes blank? Usually, candidates start writing again when an idea comes back to them and the panic is over.

Get the result!

Exam question

Why did the Provisional Government fail to survive the crisis of March to October 1917?

Tom's answer

Examiner says:

This is a good introduction. It sets the scene for this question, explains the circumstances of the Provisional Government's creation and gives a definition of 'provisional'.

It is often a good idea to explain and define some of the key words in the questions at the beginning of an essay.

The Provisional Government came to power in February 1917 as a result of a spontaneous revolution against Tsar Nicholas II. This was mainly due to the effects of the First World War in which Russia was doing badly and there were economic and social effects that seriously affected the lives of ordinary Russians. The food shortage was perhaps the most serious consequence in what was a bad winter even by Russian standards. In these circumstances the Provisional Government was not created on a firm basis and its name implies it was only a temporary government created in haste to deal with a very difficult situation.

Another factor which made the existence of the Provisional Government difficult was the fact that there were two forms of government that developed at that time. The Provisional Government was created from the Provisional Committee of the Duma. Its rival for influence was the Petrograd Soviet, which was made up of soldiers and workers. This situation continued throughout the eight months that the Provisional Government was in power.

Examiner says:

This paragraph is focused on the question and is a good example of how one paragraph can be linked to another.

However, more explanation could have been given for 'Duma' and 'Soviet'.

If the Provisional Government was going to survive, then there was a need for strong leadership to solve some of the key problems facing Russia. This provides further explanation why the Provisional Government did not survive. Firstly, the main support for the Provisional Government came from the liberals and moderate socialists, such as Kerensky who emerged as the new Prime Minister. These groups were not well equipped to deal with the difficult situation. Kerensky proved to be a good orator but ultimately made fatal errors of judgement. However, the Provisional Government was eventually overthrown in October 1917 by a Bolshevik coup d'etat led by Lenin and Trotsky who proved to be more decisive leaders who led a well-organised and determined group.

Secondly, the Provisional Government was faced with two problems that needed to be tackled: the Land question and the First World War. The Provisional Government did not deal with the land issue

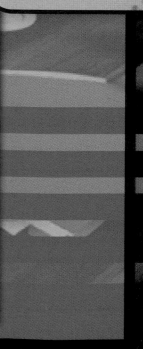

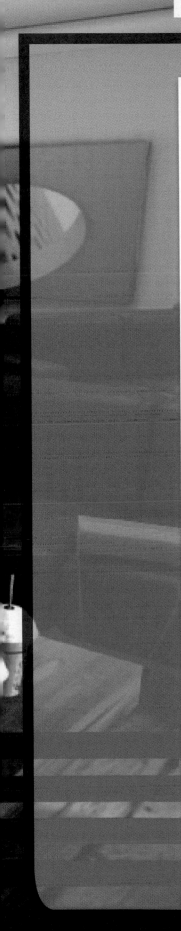

quickly enough and peasants began to seize land, which led to increasing problems in the countryside in late summer 1917. The First World War had been going badly for Russia but the Provisional Government decided to continue the war and this led to a rift with the Petrograd Soviet. This decision proved fatal because the July Offensive in Galicia ended in defeat and this led to unrest in the Ukraine and at the naval base at Kronstadt.

These two policy failures led to a loss of support for the Provisional Government. The growing unrest led to attempts to overthrow the Provisional Government. The Bolsheviks attempted to take over in July but were defeated by the Government. However, in September the Kornilov rebellion was to prove to be a decisive event in 1917. General Kornilov, who was Head of the Armed Forces, led a march on Petrograd. There has been much controversy about the motives and actions of the people involved but the crucial outcome was that Kerensky asked the left-wing Bolsheviks to help him suppress this right-wing rebellion. This strengthened the Bolsheviks who had looked a spent force after the July rebellion.

The growing strength of the Bolsheviks is the final factor in explaining why the Provisional Government failed. The Bolsheviks had played no part in the February Revolution and Lenin had arrived from exile in Switzerland in April. In June only 10% of 305 Soviets were Bolshevik. However, during late summer the Bolsheviks began to build their support by promising to solve the problems facing Russia with 'peace, bread and land'. In the September elections the majority of members of the Petrograd Soviet were Bolsheviks. The Provisional Government proved unable to cope with the October Revolution, which was a skilfully planned military coup d'etat in which the Bolsheviks seized power in Moscow and Petrograd, forcing Kerensky to flee.

Therefore, was the failure of the Provisional Government due more to the failure of Kerensky or to the skill and determination of the Bolsheviks? The failure of the Provisional Government to solve the key problems provided the main reason why the government lost the support of many people and therefore failed to survive the crisis.

Examiner says:

The last three paragraphs continue to provide a good answer to the question. They are clearly giving further reasons and are linked to each other – thus showing that a line of argument is being developed.

However, the evidence provided could be more detailed. In particular, more evaluation could be given. For example, when Tom says in the second paragraph that 'this decision proved fatal', he could have gone on to show clearly that (a) this could be a very important reason, and (b) explain why.

Examiner says:

Overall this is a very good answer that shows a clear and sound understanding of the key issues in the questions. It is well structured and has some evaluation of the reasons.

To be even better, it should have done more to explain the reasons why some factors were more important than others.

3 Issues in interpreting and evaluating sources

Sources and evidence

There is a great range of material available to and used by historians. Historians rely on literature of all kinds such as:

- official documents
- newspaper articles
- personal correspondence
- chronicles
- works of fiction.

In addition, historians frequently work with:

- figures such as statistics, e.g. population growth, economic developments
- images such as propaganda posters, cartoons in the press, film, photographs and portraits
- tangible evidence of the past in the form of landscapes, structures and other artefacts
- the skills of specialists in other fields such as mathematicians, anthropologists, geographers and archaeologists.

The subject the historian studies largely determines the sources the historian is most likely to use. Consider the example of Alfred the Great. Alfred was the king of Wessex, the great Saxon kingdom defining the south and west of Britain in the ninth century CE. The historian is restricted to the study of just two important contemporary texts concerning his reign: a biography of the king known as Asser's *Life of Alfred* and the Anglo-Saxon Chronicle, a record of English affairs written by monks, probably commissioned by Alfred himself. For Alfred, there are no newspapers, photographs, moving images or propaganda posters to consult and so the historian needs to look elsewhere.

THINK LIKE AN HISTORIAN

What other forms of evidence might be available to the historian investigating the reign of Alfred the Great?

Is it possible for historians of the reign of Alfred the Great to write a satisfactory history given the limited sources?

For discussion

How far has Figure 3.1 captured the spirit of the 1960s? What are its strengths and shortcomings as evidence for ordinary life in Britain during the period?

Figure 3.1
Montage of images representing the 1960s (cover of a CD set, c.2000).

Every historical source has value, but the historian must handle every source with care in order to derive its historical worth. Each source makes a unique contribution to the historical record, but it is also likely to bring with it a particular set of problems in its interpretation. Different types of evidence need to be approached in different ways.

Written sources

Official documents

In a world that demands 'accountability', governments and other public institutions in modern democracies are pressured into recording and making available information that can be deemed to be in 'the public interest'. In Britain much of this is available for all to consult in the **National Archives.** The range of official documents consequently is vast and spans well over a thousand years of the country's history, from before the Domesday Book to the Beveridge Report and beyond.

Although its documents fill around a hundred miles of shelving, the records are neither complete nor automatically reliable. Typically, the further the historian goes back, the sparser becomes the documentary record. Different periods pose particular problems. For example, the Tudor State Papers tend to be confined to incoming correspondence, whereas the Chancery records of earlier times are mainly copies of the government's outgoing letters and decrees and not the responses and requests, and so on, from its subjects. In some instances, for example papers relating to the **Suez Crisis** of 1956, it is evident that embarrassing or incriminating documents have been removed and, presumably, destroyed. The historian handling 'official' documents must always bear in mind the possibility that the official version of events is not necessarily the correct one or the complete one.

Official records are usually associated with political historians. However, the documents relating to the activities of generations of civil servants and other bureaucrats are of equal interest to economic and social historians. Indeed, it is often only through this evidence that we can gain a detailed understanding of the lives of ordinary people. This was amply demonstrated when the French historian, Emmanuel Le Roy Ladurie, in his book Montaillou (1978) reconstructed the lives of the illiterate peasants of a village in the French Pyrenees in the early fourteenth century through his analysis of the records of the Inquisition investigating allegations of heresy. A similar approach was taken more recently by Eamon Duffy in *Voices of Morebath* (2001), an investigation of life in a village on the Somerset-Devon border during the Reformation based upon the uniquely detailed parish records kept by its priest, Christopher Trychay. Among other things, it has shed a great deal of light on the nature of popular rebellion in the middle of the sixteenth century.

Private papers and personal writings

Private papers constitute collections of material both written by and written to the individual concerned. Such collections are invaluable to biographers, and it is not unusual for people who have played an important public role to leave this record as a legacy for the benefit of future historians. Equally, such collections reside in any number of attics in the homes of ordinary people, storing for posterity details of the lives of their equally ordinary ancestors. In both cases, historians need to be alert to the likely chance that some form of self-censorship has occurred in the assemblage of such papers as the collator of the collection decides what is worth keeping and what is not.

QUICK FACT

The **National Archives**, formerly the Public Records Office (PRO), was established in 1838. On its opening, the PRO was declared to be the central depository for 'all rolls, records, writs, books, proceedings, decrees, bills, warrants, accounts, papers, and documents whatsoever of a public nature, belonging to Her Majesty'.

QUICK FACT

In 1956, Egypt's leader, Colonel Nasser, laid claim to the Suez Canal, an important trading route which runs through Egypt and connects the Mediterranean Sea to the Red Sea. Following unsuccessful negotiations with Nasser, the British and French governments secretly backed an Israeli attack on Egypt, providing an excuse for British and French troops to occupy the canal zone in order to keep the canal open. Condemnation of their actions, particularly from the US government, forced a humiliating British and French withdrawal.

In a world before emails and telephones, the letter was the principal mode of correspondence. Of course, letters are an invaluable source for understanding social relationships in the past, but they can also greatly enhance the historian's understanding of political history. Just as modern politicians send each other regular emails, the political figures of the not-too-distant past would send each other regular, perhaps daily, letters and memos. As many politicians have found to their cost, such private correspondence is likely to be less circumspect than 'official' communications and, as such, provide wonderful insights into the thoughts of the individuals involved.

Diaries can be even more intimate than letters, particularly if they have been written without the object of anyone other than the author reading them. Plenty of public figures over the last couple of centuries have kept diaries, presumably with a view to recording events as they unfurled, and their involvement in them, for the benefit of future generations. In our own time, some eminent diarists, particularly politicians, have published their diaries within their own lifetimes. Again, the historian needs to consider carefully the diarist's purpose and the prerogative any publishing diarist has regarding the selection of what is permitted to enter the public domain. The publication of the Labour government's press chief Alastair Campbell's diary in 2007 was criticised for drawing a veil across the friction between departing Prime Minister Tony Blair and his successor Gordon Brown, and thus not providing a balanced account of the Blair government.

Arguably, the most reliable diaries are the ones that were never intended for publication. Famous diarists of the last few centuries such as Samuel Pepys (seventeenth century), Parson Woodforde (eighteenth century) and Francis Kilvert (nineteenth century) have provided wonderful insights into the mundane of the periods in which they lived: the food they ate, the clothes they wore, their interests, health, and values. Of course, a diary gives us a very individual perspective on the past which does not necessarily reflect the common experience. Furthermore, historians need to recognise the fact that until modern times such sources were the product of the literate and leisurely upper classes; the voices of the working classes of the past are less often heard, and are almost totally lost before 1800.

Newspapers

The emergence of newspapers in modern times has made the biggest contribution to providing for some subjects in some places a near-complete historical record. The first newspapers appeared in the seventeenth century. These concentrated on news of national importance, but by the late eighteenth century newspapers dedicated to local ('provincial') matters had also become established. Nowadays, of course there is a plethora of 'dailies' providing information for every group of the reading public.

When evaluating a newspaper source as evidence, the historian is confronted with the tricky issue regarding how far the newspaper reflects history and how far it *makes* it. The newspaper editorial is a powerful propaganda tool and politicians particularly are aware of the need to have national newspapers on their side in order to succeed. The transfer of support of *The Sun* from the Conservative party to Labour is said to help explain the triumphs of the latter in recent times. Newspaper articles do not always mirror public opinion and it would be naïve to assume that everything stated in a newspaper would meet the approval of its readership.

Read with care and with a keen eye for bias and an understanding of an article's purpose (for example, is it to entertain or inform?). The newspaper is an invaluable source for the historian of more modern times.

Novels

The novel, like other forms of creative expression such as paintings, poetry, pop-songs and screenplays, is usually the product of a single mind, and offers a personal view. Furthermore, to a greater or lesser degree, the novel is a work of fiction; it tells a story and, ultimately, it is designed to 'entertain', in the broadest sense of the term, in order to sell copies. Often it distorts or oversimplifies the truth to make a point or perhaps simply 'for effect'. As such, it can be a particularly problematic source of evidence for the historian in search of 'facts'.

However, the novel, emerging as an art form in the eighteenth century, is an important and fascinating subject of historical study. It is the product of the times in which it is written and, whatever the subject matter, be it science-fiction or historical, even the most skilful novelist is unable to shed all vestiges of the culture of the age in which the novel is written. The same can be said of historians. Sometimes, issues of great contemporary interest underpin the novel: shortly before Emile Durkheim launched the craft of modern sociology with his classic work *Suicide* (1897) in England, Thomas Hardy's last novel, *Jude the Obscure* (1895), was centred on the same theme – the degeneracy of the modern industrial world as debated by the statisticians, doctors and **Social-Darwinians** across Europe at that time. In much the same way, George Orwell reflected public concerns in his gloomy 'distopian' vision of the future, *Nineteen Eighty-Four*, at the start of the **Cold War**.

Oral accounts and personal histories

Oral history is fallible on two counts: it is determined by what the subject tells the interviewer and what the interviewer asks the subject. Memories are imperfect and people can unintentionally, sometimes intentionally, distort past truths. Interviewers may have an agenda that shapes the interview and they cannot be relied upon to be entirely objective when making the results of the interview available to a wider audience. Recollections, arguably, are less reliable than contemporaneous sources of evidence since people's memories are not infallible. Furthermore, eyewitness accounts of the past are not necessarily any more truthful than the statements of witnesses in courts of law.

However, the oral account is now recognised as a very important historical source. The popularisation of the approach coincided with the widening availability of the technology by which accounts could be recorded and it is now an activity with which anyone interested in the past can easily get involved. Indeed, it must be the simplest and most direct way in which a researcher can acquire a bank of unique and previously unrecorded source material.

The earliest compilations of oral history date to the nineteenth century when Diana Maria Mulock in her *Unsentimental Journey through Cornwall* (1884) recorded the accounts of local people, accounts that up to this point were likely to be lost to the historical record. It can be argued that this kind of record is all the more important than 'elite' oral history since the famous are far more likely to leave their mark for posterity in other places. Not surprisingly, therefore, the technique has proved particularly useful to the writers of the history of women's lives in recent times.

Major projects have been undertaken, including a study in the 1970s by Paul Thompson and Essex University of Edwardian life based upon the systematic interviewing of 500 people from a broad range of backgrounds with memories stretching back at least as far as 1911. Another very important, ongoing project is the compilation of the Imperial War Museum's Sound Archive. This massive collection of recorded interviews has been compiled over 30 years and contains recollections of all of the major conflicts in which Britain has been involved since the Second Boer War (1899–1902).

QUICK FACT

Social-Darwinians applied Darwin's laws of evolutionary theory to competition within, and between, human societies. Darwin's theories were used sometimes to justify racist ideologies in the first half of the twentieth century.

QUICK FACT

The **Cold War** defines the period of international tension between 1945–46 and 1989. During this time, the dire threat of nuclear weaponry helped prevent the clash between the ideologies of US-style capitalism and the communism of the Soviet Union from erupting into a third world war.

Visual sources

Maps

Matthew Paris, a thirteenth-century Benedictine monk, is credited with the first English map of the British Isles. By the early fourteenth century, maps accompanied local surveys, and by the end of that century 'town views' were being made for a variety of purposes. Most British towns have at least one map dating from the eighteenth century or earlier. The explosion of commerce in the eighteenth and nineteenth centuries produced detailed road maps and traveller guides. The first Ordnance Survey map appeared in 1801. These detailed, accurate maps started life as maps designed for military purposes during the Napoleonic Wars. Since then, it has become a service for the benefit of the public and the government alike. Modern maps are precision objects of great accuracy. Older maps are not and some are little more than works of geographical fiction! Nevertheless, even these are of value as evidence of the ways in which people in the past have pictured their world.

Figure 3.2 shows a thirteenth-century map of the world known as the 'mappa mundi'. It can be found in Hereford Cathedral and was used for educational purposes. Although reasonably accurate in some respects, it is wildly fanciful in others, for example its images of mythical creatures associated with various parts of the world. These include one-legged humanoids with a single huge foot to shade them from the sun in far-off hot lands! Following an ancient convention which portrayed the world as a circle with Rome at the centre, at the very centre of this map is the city of Jerusalem. At the top of the map is the image of Christ on the Day of Judgement, turning away sinners but admitting the repentant and righteous into Heaven.

THINK LIKE AN HISTORIAN

The 'mappa mundi' is of limited use to a modern-day geographer, but of immense value to historians of the medieval period.

What can historians learn from the 'mappa mundi'?

▌ **Figure 3.2**
'Mappa mundi', a map of the world made in England, c.1290.

Maps are an essential tool for any historian navigating their way through the past, and both modern and historical maps are excellent sources of evidence in their own right. Old maps provide evidence for detailed developments that are likely to have eluded other documentary records.

Modern maps are also hugely useful in illuminating the past. The shape of field boundaries and roads can indicate the site of structures that no longer exist. Isolated churches may well mark the site of villages deserted perhaps in the aftermath of the Black Death or as a consequence of large-scale enclosures. Street names can reveal the activities formerly associated with specific areas in towns and villages, and the names of whole settlements themselves can reveal the presence of foreign settlers in early times. Some fascinating studies, for example, have been undertaken into the spread of Scandinavian-influenced place names to show the impact of Viking settlement from the ninth century; the suffixes -thorpe and -by are almost exclusively found to the north of the boundary that separated the areas under the Danelaw from the Anglo-Saxon kingdoms of central and southern Britain – see Figure 3.3.

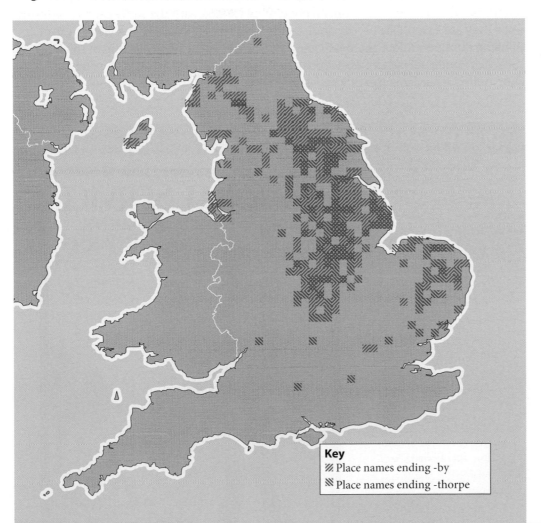

Key
Place names ending -by
Place names ending -thorpe

▌ **Figure 3.3**
Distribution of place names in England of Scandinavian origin. The suffix -by meant a farmstead while -thorpe indicated a small extra or overflow settlement

Cartoons and posters

Political cartoons in newspapers, despite being the artist's personal view on a contemporary theme, can usually be relied upon to reflect the attitude of the readership it caters for. Unlike the work of the modern historian, the work of the cartoonist is openly opinionated and designed to provoke an emotional, rather than an intellectual, response. A cartoon that works is one that angers the reader or makes the reader laugh. Cartoons rarely provide a literal truth, but the most useful ones give a direct and succinct insight into the concerns of a time and place regarding some contentious issue. It is their very subjectivity, their bias, that makes them such important sources of evidence. The fact that they tend to use metaphors to make points, that they can grossly exaggerate the truth, and that they sometimes rely on irony, however, can make them problematic sources for historians; without a good knowledge of the historical context in which they appeared, the historian is likely to miss the cartoon's point entirely.

Other visual **polemical sources** include political posters, advertisements and party political broadcasts on television. All need to be treated with the same care as cartoons since they are essentially propagandist – their object is to provoke the viewer into thinking about a subject and persuading the viewer into a particular line of thinking. As such, it is immensely useful as evidence; even propaganda that lies is of value in illuminating a particular set of values current in a particular place and time.

Polemical sources

Sources that may be controversial.

EXAM TIP

When presented with an overtly propagandist source, do not dismiss it out of hand as 'unreliable' even if it does not 'tell the truth'! It gives you a direct insight into the way one group of people was thinking in the past.

THINK LIKE AN HISTORIAN

Consider the questions below and then write a paragraph on the value of this poster as historical evidence.

1. What is the purpose of this British poster?

2. What is its target audience?

3. How does it depict life in the Women's Land Army?

4. For what reasons might a young woman find reality very different to that portrayed?

5. Does propaganda like this intentionally lie or mislead?

6. Does this undermine this poster's value as historical evidence?

■ Figure 3.4
A First World War National Service poster

Statistics

'There are three kinds of lies: lies, damned lies, and statistics.' (Mark Twain quoting, he believed, Benjamin Disraeli)

Statistics have a central role in historical enquiries. The political or social historian uses them as much as the economic in their investigations of such matters as voting patterns, the growth of literacy and industrial development. They need to be handled with care since the results are only as reliable as the methods by which the statistics were gathered. **Enumerators** make mistakes and do sometimes lie.

Even when the results can be considered trustworthy, it is easy for historians to misinterpret them. A major debate in British economic history surrounds the impact of the Industrial Revolution upon the standard of living. In 1957, the historian R. B. Hobsbawm in 'The British Standard of Living in England, 1800–50' 'proved' that the standard of living for working people in London was falling because meat sales at the Smithfield market fell during the period – meat being the item most indicative of prosperity in any working-class shopping basket in the nineteenth century. R. M. Hartwell (1961) in 'The Rising Standard of Living in England, 1800–50' challenged Hobsbawm's conclusion by focusing on the evidence for the Increased sale of meat in other markets and also by considering the consumption of fish. As the debate progressed, E. P. Thompson (1967) pointed out that the standard of living cannot be measured in a purely quantitative manner; the *quality* of life is of equal or even greater importance. It seems that the issue can never be resolved by statistics alone.

B. R. Mitchell (1994) in an interesting article on the subject highlighted the danger of reading too much into percentage increase or decrease when handling statistics: 'A 1000% rise in (say) Bulgarian steel output over five years may seem huge and highly significant – until it is pointed out that the initial output was minute.'

In a similar vein the nineteenth-century English wit and satirist Sydney Smith lampooned the panic that gripped the country when cholera struck again in 1848:

> **Enumerator**
>
> Someone who collects data, e.g. a commissioner employed to fill in census information through a house-to-house survey.

Source (1)

Cholera made one successful effort at Taunton and not repeated it though a month has elapsed…The cholera will have killed by the end of the year about one person in every thousand. Therefore it is a thousand to one (supposing the cholera to travel at the same rate) that any person does not die of the cholera in any one year. This calculation is for the mass, but if you are prudent, temperate and rich your chance is at least five times as good that you do not die of cholera; in other words 5000 to 1. And if it is 5000 to 1 that you do not die of cholera in a year, it is not far from two million to one that you do not die any one day of cholera.'

Sydney Smith

In percentage terms the increased incidence of cholera in 1848 was enormous since it had not occurred since 1832, but in terms of the mortality rate, the impact, at least in Taunton, was minimal. Smith's comments also highlight the problem of generalisation: what might be a statistical 'truth' for one group of people is not necessarily true for another.

Photographs

The photograph is another unique source for the study of recent history. An invention of the first half of the nineteenth century, photography has played a key role in shaping our understanding of the world since the 1850s. As evidence, early photos can be limited since shutter speeds necessitated carefully posed 'unnatural' settings of people and they tended to record the lives and interests of the more privileged. By the end of the nineteenth century, however, the camera was recording most aspects of life, including industrial work and warfare.

▌ **Figure 3.5**
Lenin addressing a crowd in Moscow in May 1920.

As with other sources of evidence, the historian needs to consider the context in which the image was captured. The principle consideration is what motivated the photographer to take that particular photograph in the first place. Political history of the twentieth century is littered with photographs that served a purely propagandist purpose. Of course, this does not make a photograph less valuable, but it does highlight how important it is to avoid falling into the trap of taking a photograph at 'face value'. Furthermore, with digital technology it has become easy to manipulate and falsify images. This has been going on for a long time – 'doctored' photographs from the Edwardian period, for example, survive purporting to show fairies and ghosts. After he achieved full control over the USSR by the late 1920s, Stalin had his archrival Trotsky 'airbrushed' from photographs that revealed the latter's central role in the Bolshevik Revolution of 1917. In Figure 3.5 the photo above shows the Bolshevik leader, Lenin, addressing a crowd of supporters – Trotsky is the figure in military uniform to the right of the podium. Now compare it with the almost identical image below.

How, and why, do these pictures differ?

Primary and secondary sources

Historians handle both a huge amount and a wide range of evidence. Dealing with evidence effectively necessitates ordering the evidence. As well as dividing evidence by type, historians divide evidence into primary and secondary sources. These terms are determined by the historian's purpose. For example, if a historian is trying to discover what happened in 871 CE, when Alfred the Great was attacked by the Vikings, the contemporary accounts of the events, written down by the people who lived through them are the primary sources, whereas the accounts of these events written by subsequent historians are the secondary sources. Thus Asser's *Life of Alfred* and the Anglo-Saxon Chronicle, mentioned earlier, are primary sources for this purpose. However, if the historian decides to explore how the popular image of Alfred the Great has changed over time, the subsequent historical accounts also become primary sources. The focus of the historian's attention is no longer just on the events of the ninth century. It is equally concerned with the events of the Tudor, Stuart, Georgian and Victorian periods that helped shape the interpretation of those who wrote about Alfred in those periods.

THINK LIKE AN HISTORIAN

Try grouping the following into primary and secondary sources for the history of Victorian education:

a) David Vincent (1981) *Bread, Knowledge and Freedom: a study of nineteenth century working class autobiography*

b) Charles Shaw, *When I was a Child* (first published in 1903)

c) *Kilvert's Diary* (the diary of a Victorian clergyman interested in education, first published in 1944)

d) Harold Silver (1975) *Education and the Radicals 1780–1850*

e) Marjorie Reeves (1978) *Sheep Bell and Ploughshare: the story of two village families* [from the late seventeenth to the early twentieth centuries]

f) *Journal of a Somerset Rector* (the journal of a clergyman and supervisor of a Sunday School who died shortly after the start of the reign of Queen Victoria, first published in 1930)

g) Victorian print showing a 'ragged' school (see Figure 3.6).

What type of source is this book as evidence for the study of education since Victorian times – a primary or a secondary source?

■ Figure 3.6
A Victorian print showing a 'ragged' school

How to read sources

Whether studying Alfred the Great or Victorian education or, for that matter, any other subject, research historians are most likely to spend the greatest amount of their time working with written sources. At AS and A2 Level you will usually be given sources that have been carefully selected, and if necessary translated or put into modern English, in order to make them appropriate for this stage of your studies. However, you are bound to come across words, phrases and references that you find difficult to make sense of. A dictionary and a reliable historical encyclopaedia are essential tools for the historian engaging with documentary sources.

Before reading a source, start by working out what sort of source you are dealing with. In the exam, this will be made clear in the preamble and footnotes for the source. You should be able to identify very rapidly:

- WHEN the source was written
- WHO wrote the source
- WHAT type of source it is.

If you are lucky you may even have been given enough information to discover WHY the source was written before you read it.

Fines' first five steps to success

A very influential modern teacher of history teachers, John Fines, devised an eight-stage approach to the study of any written source. These are the first five and they are as good a place as any to start in the structured analysis of a document – see Figure 3.7.

Step 1	**Describe the document – is it a diary extract, an official form, a newspaper article?**
Step 2	**What information does it contain regarding such things as people, places, time, ideas?**
Step 3	**What difficult words, phrases and references does it contain?** **Use a dictionary, encyclopaedia, atlas, etc. to develop your understanding.**
Step 4	**Read the source again. What words or phrases (if any) help give away the period in which the source was written. This might be reflected in the attitudes of the writer regarding such things as religion and political ideas, or the absence of 'hindsight' (i.e. knowledge of what happened afterwards) as much as it is evident in any archaic language.**
Step 5	**How reliable is the source? Identify anything that is of dubious reliability because, for example, there is a lack of supporting evidence for a claim, or the source clearly is biased. Look out for any words or phrases which are particularly emotive, subjective, opinionated.**

▌ **Figure 3.7**
The first five stages in the study of written sources

Adapted from J. Fines (1988) *Reading Historical Documents*, Basil Blackwell.

The four Ws

When analysing sources, remember to ask yourself the four Ws:

- When was the source written?
- Who wrote the source?
- What type of source is it?
- Why was the source written?

THINK LIKE AN HISTORIAN

Try applying Fines' first five steps to Source 2, a series of extracts from Prime Minister Neville Chamberlain's speech on the day that Britain declared war on Germany.

Source 2

This repeated disregard of his word and these sudden reversals of policy bring me to the fundamental difficulty in dealing with the wider proposals in the German Chancellor's speech. The plain truth is that, after our past experience, it is no longer possible to rely upon the unsupported word of the present German Government.

It was not therefore with any vindictive purpose that we embarked on war. It is not alone the freedom of the small nations that is at stake: there is also in jeopardy the peaceful existence of Great Britain, the Dominions, France, and indeed of all freedom-loving countries. Whatever may be the issue of the present struggle, and in whatever way it may be brought to a conclusion, the world will not be the same world that we have known before. Deep changes will inevitably leave their mark on every field of men's thought and action, and if humanity is to guide aright the new forces that will be in operation all nations will have their part to play.

His Majesty's Government know all too well that in modern war between great Powers victor and vanquished must alike suffer cruel loss. But surrender to wrong-doing would spell the extinction of all hope, and the annihilation of all those values of life which have through centuries been at once the mark and the inspiration of human progress.

I am certain that all the peoples of Europe, including the people of Germany, long for peace, a peace which will enable them to live their lives without fear, and to devote their energies and their gifts to the development of their culture, the pursuit of their ideals and the improvement of their material prosperity. The peace which we are determined to secure, however, must be a real and settled peace, not an uneasy truce interrupted by constant alarms and repeated threats. What stands in the way of such a peace? It is the German Government, and the German Government alone for it is they

who by repeated acts of aggression have robbed all Europe of tranquillity and implanted in the hearts of all their neighbours an ever-present sense of insecurity and fear.

Herr Hitler rejected all suggestions for peace until he had overwhelmed Poland, as he had previously overthrown Czechoslovakia. Peace conditions cannot be acceptable which begin by condoning aggression. The proposals in the German Chancellor's speech are vague and uncertain and contain no suggestion for righting the wrongs done to Czechoslovakia and to Poland. Even if Herr Hitler's proposals were more closely defined and contained suggestions to right these wrongs, it would still be necessary to ask by what practical means the German Government intend to convince the world that aggression will cease and that pledges will be kept. Past experience has shown that no reliance can be placed upon the promises of the present German Government. Accordingly, acts not words alone must be forthcoming before we and France, our gallant and trusted ally, would be justified in ceasing to wage war to the utmost of our strength. Only when world confidence is restored will it be possible to find solutions of those vital questions of disarmament and restoration of trade which are essential to the well-being of the peoples.

There is thus a primary condition to be satisfied. Only the German Government can fulfil it. If they will not, there can as yet be no new or better world order of the kind for which all nations yearn.

The issue is therefore plain. Either the German Government must give convincing proof of the sincerity of their desire for peace by definite acts and by the provision of effective guarantees of their intention to fulfil their undertakings or we must persevere in our duty to the end. It is for Germany to make her choice.

Neville Chamberlain, 3 September 1939

EXAM TIP

Take a highlighter pen into every exam. It is an excellent tool for the analysis of sources. Two colours are better than one, for example if you need to identify points of similarity and difference between two sources. If this is your own book, use a highlighter as you work through the various activities in this section.

EXAM TIP

Do not undervalue sources in an examination. The sources you are asked to analyse have been very carefully chosen for the subject in hand and you can be certain that they have great value and relevance to the topic. The examiner will not be impressed if you dismiss these unique sources as worthless!

Once you have finished analysing the source, you will be in a position to consider its worth as historical evidence. Obviously, the value of the source will depend on the historian's purpose. Try answering the following questions:

1. Of what value is this source as evidence for an historian investigating:

   a) the policy of the British government towards Germany between 1937 and 1939

   b) the reasons why Britain went to war in 1939

   c) the British government's war aims in 1939

   d) the mood of public opinion in Britain in 1939?

2. For which of these is the source most useful? For which of these is it least useful? Why?

Context

When an archaeologist is asked to assess a find, the first thing they will want to know about is the context in which it was found – if it has been dug up and there is detailed information of where it lay in the ground, in which layer or 'strata' of the site, it will be of far more value to the archaeologist than if that information has been lost and the object is 'unstratified'. To the archaeologist and the historian alike, context is crucial and evidence cannot be fully understood without it.

Historians use a term that takes centre stage in the world of antique dealers to describe the concept of context: **provenance**. This brings us back to the four Ws – who, when, where, why (see above). The provenance of the source is all to do with the time and place in which the document was written, in which the painting was painted, in which the interview was recorded. For historians, it is the metaphorical 'layer' in their excavation of the past.

EXAM TIP

Whenever you are asked questions like this, you must fully expplain your answer. Always remember that the academic discipline of history is to do with the forming of interpretation based upon the analysing of evidence. Without evidence historians' statements are merly unproven hypothesis and of little value.

Provenance

The origin and purpose of a source.

■ **Figure 3.8**
This drawing is based upon the *stratigraphy* of an archaeological excavation. It shows, as a cross-section, layers, identified by an archaeologist. These reveal phases of human activity at this site from the Iron Age to the present

Stratigraphy

The study by archaeologists of the soil layers (strata) in which objects are found.

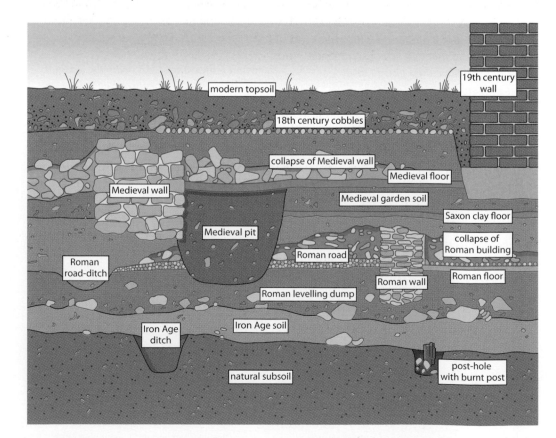

modern topsoil

19th century wall

18th century cobbles

collapse of Medieval wall

Medieval floor

Medieval wall

Medieval garden soil

Saxon clay floor

Medieval pit

collapse of Roman building

Roman road

Roman road-ditch

Roman wall

Roman floor

Roman levelling dump

Iron Age soil

Iron Age ditch

natural subsoil

post-hole with burnt post

ACTIVITY

Look at Figure 3.8. Working from the bottom to the top, summarise the evolution of this site. Look carefully at how later layers cut into earlier layers. (Note: the Iron Age ditch and post hole probably indicate a house structure with a surrounding drainage gully.)

Explain why the broken pot in the medieval pit would be of less value to the archaeologist without knowledge of the context in which it was found.

Use this diagram as an analogy for explaining to someone in your class the importance of context in the analysis of historical documents.

Hypotheses

Since the start of the twentieth century, there has been a debate among academics concerning the question, 'Is History a science?' A nineteenth-century German historian, Leopold von Ranke, maintained that it is a science because historians employ, or should employ, a scientific method in the pursuit of historical facts. As in the natural sciences, he maintained, historians' results are the outcome of formulating and testing hypotheses. (For more information on hypotheses, see Chapter 1 The nature of historical explanation, page 3.)

Academic history is more than the mere chronicling of events. Historians ask questions in order to understand what happened and why. When they envisage an answer to the question, they form a hypothesis. The hypothesis can then be 'tested' by examining further evidence in order to establish whether or not it is correct, whether it needs modification or whether it should be abandoned.

Of course, the evidence available is usually incomplete, sometimes hard to make sense of and often contradictory. Historians reach their conclusions about the past on the basis of what seems most likely in the light of their understanding of the available evidence. In so doing, they should endeavour to be as *objective* as possible.

Counterfactual method

Another approach to trying to understand the past is the 'What if?' approach or **counterfactual method**. Quite simply, historians can consider how things might have occurred if something had happened differently in the past. It is something we all consider at times in our personal lives, particularly when we draw the conclusion 'If only…!' As often as not we are best advised to forget the 'What ifs' and get on with things as they are. Likewise, some historians consider the counterfactual approach to history counterproductive.

However, serious historical studies of some worth have been based on the counterfactual method. A good example, though now discredited, is Robert Fogel's *The Railroads and American Economic Growth* (1964) in which he endeavoured to quantify the importance of the railway in America's industrial development by considering how things might have turned out without it. He arrived at the conclusion that without the railway, and hence reliance on other means of transport, the net loss to America during the period of its industrial revolution would have been no more than 4 per cent of its national income.

While a reliance on the counterfactual method to reach specific conclusions might be foolhardy, historians can scarcely avoid the 'What if?' approach entirely. For example, with any study of causation the historian consciously or subconsciously considers whether a series of events might still have occurred as they did if any one possible causal factor were to be removed. This is a particularly valuable technique when trying

For discussion

In a small group, discuss:

(a) To what extent historians can be entirely objective in their analysis of the past?

(b) How might an historian's personality and life experience affect the history they write?

to understand how one thing led to another and the significance of a particular event or trend. Consider the case of the outbreak of the Second World War, for example. What if Hitler had been killed in Munich when he attempted to overthrow the government in 1923? Would German democracy still have given way to dictatorship, totalitarianism and war in the 1930s? Such is the reasoning of the historian grappling with the issue of how far any one individual could have provoked such a profound and colossal event as a world war.

Source 3 is an extract from a book that attempts to recreate life in Britain as it might have been had Germany won the Second World War. All of the Nazis mentioned were real people and the author, Comer Clarke (1962), claims that his account is 'carefully based on Nazi plans and testimony … and upon our official preparations to resist'.

THINK LIKE AN HISTORIAN

Was anything in the past bound to happen, that is, 'inevitable'? Think of five major events in human history and consider if a slightly different set of circumstances might have prevented them.

Source ③

Obersturmbannfuehrer Fritz Knoechlein, of the Second Infantry Regiment of the Totenkopf (Death's Head) Division of the Waffen SS, sat at his desk in his office in Whitehall. A swastika, black in its circle of white on a red background, hung loosely from its standard in the far corner of the room.

Beside him Sturmbannfuehrer Heinz Lammerding, immaculate in the black uniform of the Totenkopf, assumed the tight-lipped expression of his chief. Handsome, 30-year-old Fritz Knoechlein looked at Lammerding and stabbed a finger heavily on the report before him.

'This is the reason,' he said, 'that we have been drafted to England. This is the third attack on a German soldier this week. This time it has happened in a village called Chalfont St Giles. The Wehrmacht [German army] has questioned all the villagers, but none of them will say who is responsible… This has got to stop and we are empowered by Himmler to act… These people who attack the German occupying forces must

learn that they cannot trifle with the Waffen SS.'

… Knoechlein walked to the window and looked out into Whitehall. This was London. German occupied London. For in September 1940, with the Continent on its knees, Hitler's blitzkrieg [lightning war] had been launched upon Britain.

The mighty Luftwaffe had finally tipped the scales against the valiant Royal Air Force which had held Britain's fate in the balance for so many desperate weeks. By sea and air the troops and parachutists of Operation 'Sea Lion' which was Hitler's code name for the invasion of Britain, had flooded in… In the weeks of ferocity and violence which no Briton thought could happen, London, then the rest of Britain, fell as in that terrible summer of 1940 the other countries of Europe had fallen to the armed might of Nazi Germany.

…Yes it had happened.
The Nazis had come.

C. Clarke (1962) *If the Nazis had Come*,
Consul Books.

For discussion

In a small group, discuss whether Clarke's work (source 3) should be considered 'history' or, at least, 'historical'.

Is an exercise of this sort of any real value to the historian of the era of the Second World War? Is it of any real value to the historian of the late 1950s/early 1960s?

Regressive method

The hypothetical approach detailed above relied upon a considerable number of documentary sources and oral accounts. The **regressive method** is another approach to understanding the past, typically employed when documentary evidence is lacking. The basic principle works on the assumption that from our knowledge of a particular time and place, we can infer something of what went before. Practitioners of the method, in the words of a great nineteenth-century historian, F. W. Maitland, work 'backwards from the known to the unknown, from the certain to the uncertain'. This approach is of particular relevance to the historians of issues for which few documentary sources have survived. It has been employed, for example, in the reconstruction of population history of England and Wales before the introduction of the Census (1801) or the compulsory recording of baptisms, marriages and funerals in parish registers (1538). The method relies upon the assumption that history is a continuum – that elements of the past can always be found in the present. Landscape historians employ this approach when they consult modern maps and attempt to reveal the geography of the past through the examination of such things as modern field boundaries and place names.

Summary

- Historians rely on a very wide range of sources. Documentary sources include:

  Written sources

  – official documents

  – private papers and personal writings

  – newspapers

  – novels

  – oral accounts and personal histories.

  Visual sources

  – maps

  – cartoons and posters

  – statistics

  – photographs.

- Historians sometimes group sources into 'primary' and 'secondary' sources. These definitions depend upon the historian's purpose.

- When analysing sources historians are interested in:

  – WHEN it was written

  – WHO wrote it

  – WHAT sort of source it is

  – WHY it was written.

- The most effective approach to the analysis of sources is a systematic approach such as that devised by John Fines.

- It is as crucial for the historian to understand the context in which a source was produced as it is for the archaeologist to know where in the ground an artefact was recovered.

- Like scientists, historians ask questions, form hypotheses and use historical evidence to arrive at interpretations.

- Sometimes historians evaluate the significance of something in the past by considering what would have happened if it was absent. This 'What if?' approach is known as the counterfactual method.

- In the absence of evidence historians sometimes employ a regressive method to try to find out about the past.

For discussion

In a small group, discuss the main strengths and weaknesses of the counterfactual and regressive approaches to the study of the past.

4 The application of the theory

Constructing and evaluating historical interpretations

This section comprises six case studies based upon some of the options available for examination in the OCR GCE AS History Syllabus B Using Historical Evidence, Units F983/F984. For each there is a short introduction providing an outline of the relevant narrative. The case studies have been designed to be studied without the need for previous knowledge of the topic. The activities linked to the sources develop the skills essential for success in the study of historical evidence while at the same time introducing a variety of interesting themes.

Case study 1: The Vikings in Europe, 790s–1066

Introduction

The full comprehension of any source relies on some knowledge and understanding of the context in which it was written. In the case of the Vikings, it is all-important in explaining why a whole culture has been popularly and erroneously remembered as uniquely violent and barbaric. Try an internet image search for the word 'Viking' and it will produce a listing dominated by pictures of men in horned helmets wielding a variety of gruesome looking weapons, typically sailing in or disembarking from longships. The recent 'Asterix and the Vikings' film is no exception to the general rule and helps perpetuate the myth for another generation – see source 1.

> ### EXAM TIP
>
> The effective analysis of a set of sources can be compared to the baking of a perfect cake or the mixing of a great track. The result is a successful synthesis, be it of tastes and textures, sounds, or historical information.
>
> In the analysis of historical documents, synthesis, which means blending things together, necessitates cross-referencing sources and considering them in the context of your own knowledge.

Source 1   Twenty-first century Vikings

A still from the cartoon film 'Asterix and the Vikings' (2006). There is no historical or archaeological evidence to suggest Vikings ever wore horned helmets!

Why is it that such a one-dimensional image of this people, despite ample evidence for their highly sophisticated and multi-faceted culture, should have survived for a thousand years? The answer lies in the purpose of those who have commented on the Vikings in the past and the context in which their comments were made.

The first detailed historical records that concern the Vikings were made not by themselves but by the people with whom they made contact. Source 2, for example, is an early entry concerning the Viking attacks on Britain as recorded by the Anglo-Saxon Chronicle.

Source 2 Eighth-century Vikings

793 CE. In this year fierce, foreboding omens came over the land of Northumbria, and wretchedly terrified the people. There were excessive whirlwinds, lightning storms, and fiery dragons were seen flying in the sky. These signs were followed by great famine, and shortly after in the same year, on January 8th, the ravaging of heathen men destroyed God's church at Lindisfarne through brutal robbery and slaughter…

From the Anglo-Saxon Chronicle

How reliable is source 2?

Does it tell us more about the Vikings or the attitude of the writer?

For a man like Alfred the Great, driven by his Christian faith, the scourge of the Vikings, ultimately, had to be regarded as a punishment from God for the sins of the Anglo-Saxons. The Anglo-Saxon Chronicle was almost certainly commissioned by Alfred the Great in around 890 CE. It served a political purpose at a time when Alfred was keen to develop a sense of national (that is, Saxon) and Christian unity in his struggle against Viking attacks on his kingdom of Wessex – by this time, the Vikings had already conquered the whole of the north and east of England.

The term 'Viking' is thought to derive from the Norse word *vik* meaning a creek or inlet. The word therefore is wrapped up with the concept of a seafaring people, of people making contact through sea-borne trade or, more ominously, piracy. This aspect of their lives, as opposed to all of the other things they did, such as farming, fishing and craftwork, has come to define the Scandinavians of early medieval Europe.

The monkish chroniclers were far more likely to record violent acts of piracy, particularly when churches and churchmen were attacked, than the peaceful trading that no doubt continued throughout the era of the Viking raids.

How might the perpetuation of the image of Vikings as ruthless, bloodthirsty, heathen invaders have helped Alfred's cause?

Source ③ The Vikings in France in the 840s

843 CE. Pirates of the Northmen's race came to Nantes, killed the bishop and many of the clergy and laymen, both men and women, and pillaged the city. Thence they set out to plunder the lands of lower Aquitaine. At length they arrived at a certain island [the isle of Rhé], and carried materials thither from the mainland to build themselves houses; and they settled there for the winter, as if that were to be their permanent dwelling-place.

From the contemporary Annals of St Bertin

Sometimes chroniclers exaggerated to make an impact. In an age of mass illiteracy, the chronicles were designed to be read aloud for the entertainment as well as the education of an audience.

Source ④ The Vikings in France in the 860s

The number of ships increases, the endless flood never ceases to grow bigger. Everywhere Christ's People are the victims of massacre, burning, and plunder. The Vikings over run all that lies before them, and none can withstand them. They seize Bordeaux, Perigueux, Limoges, Angouleme, Toulouse; Angers, Tours and Orleans are made deserts. Ships past counting voyage up the Seine, and throughout the entire region evil grows strong. Rouen is laid waste, looted and burnt: Paris, Beauvais, Meaux are taken. Melun's stronghold is razed to the ground, Chartres occupied, Evreux and Bayeux looted, and every town invested.

From the contemporary account of Ermentarius of Noirmoutier

For discussion

What words and phrases have been used in source 4 to heighten the drama of the Viking presence in France in the 860s?

When Scandinavian writers like Snorri Sturluson began to write down their legendary history in the form of twelfth- and thirteenth-century sagas, they too favoured the dramatic – stories of blood-feuds, warfare, adventures abroad and seafaring. Gripping stories they most certainly are, accurate histories they are not.

Source ⑤ An extract from a Viking saga

There was a man who ran up to Kari's side, and meant to cut off his leg, but Bjorn cut off that man's arm, and sprang back again behind Kari, and they could not do him any hurt. Kari made a sweep at that same man with his sword, and cut him asunder at the waist. Then Lambi Sigfus' son rushed at Kari, and hewed at him with his sword. Kari caught the blow sideways on his shield, and the sword would not bite; then Kari thrust at Lambi with his sword just below the breast, so that the point came out between his shoulders, and that was his deathblow.

From Njal's Saga, first written down in the thirteenth century

Despite frequent scenes of violence and cruelty, the sagas represent the earliest writings in western Europe that celebrated rather than condemned Viking culture. Where Saxon monks had identified demons, the writers of the sagas found heroes.

Archaeology in modern times has helped to develop a more positive view of Vikings, not least through the discovery of the remains of their superb longships. For one British translator of Viking sagas, the dramatic achievements of technologically advanced and expansionist, 'imperialistic' Vikings of the ninth century had parallels with the world of British engineers and entrepreneurs of the nineteenth – see Source 6.

Source 6   Nineteenth-century Vikings

They were like England in the nineteenth century: fifty years before all the rest of the world with her manufactories and firms – and twenty years before them in railways. They were foremost in the race of civilisation and progress; well started before all the rest had thought of running. No wonder therefore that both won.

Quoted in J. Richards (2001) *Blood of the Vikings*, Hodder & Stoughton, p. 8

Whereas in the eighteenth century, the legacy of the classical world was celebrated by the north and west European nations, in the nineteenth it was largely superseded by pride in their common Nordic/Germanic/'Gothic' ancestry. Eventually, in Germany this shift would become an important element in a particular brand of north European nationalism: National Socialism, the politics of the Nazis.

Source 7

Twentieth-century Vikings

The German people were suggested as being descendants of the Aryans, a race of superior people who were responsible for all mankind's great achievements. It was only a small step to identify the already mythologised Vikings with this pure Germanic race. This association was developed further by Adolf Hitler and the Nazi Party after the German defeat in World War I…The name Viking was co-opted for a regiment of Norwegian volunteers and Nazi propaganda often featured the Viking image.

J. Richards (2001)
Blood of the Vikings,
Hodder & Stoughton, pp. 9 –10.

Source 8

Blood of the Vikings?

A Nazi recruiting poster produced during the German occupation of Norway in the Second World War. The poster reads 'With the Waffen SS, the Norwegian Legion fights the enemy… Communism'

THINK LIKE AN HISTORIAN

Consider sources 1–8 as a set. Work through the following exercises to test the validity of this interpretation:

The Viking myth reflects the contexts in which they have been written about in the past more than it reflects historical fact.

1. Explain how far the sources support this interpretation. You may, if you wish, amend the interpretation or suggest a different interpretation. If you do this, you must use the sources to support the changes you make.

EXAM TIP

Remember not to simply take the sources at face value. Use your knowledge of the period to interpret and evaluate them.

2. Explain how these sources are both useful and raise problems and issues for an historian using them.

EXAM TIP

Before submitting your answer to the questions above and moving on to the next case study, use the checklist below to make sure you have taken the right approach for a top grade.

If this is your own book, put ticks in the boxes as appropriate. Remember, the job isn't done until all the boxes have been filled.

The key areas checklist may be printed out from the CD-ROM.

Key areas checklist

Knowledge and understanding	Interpretation of sources	Historical interpretations
To tick this box, you need to have revealed some additional knowledge of the topic (use the introductory section for this) and shown an understanding of developments over time. Your answer should be structured around key themes and divided into separate paragraphs for each.	To tick this box, you need to have considered the provenance of the sources, and how it affects their content, in your evaluation. Your answer will have plenty of cross-referencing of sources as opposed to a simple evaluation of each source in isolation.	To tick this box, you need to have shown that you understand how interpretations are limited to the available evidence. You will have appreciated the limitations of the small amount of evidence you have analysed and so your conclusion will be based in part upon your own knowledge.
Achieved?	Achieved?	Achieved?

Case study 2: The impact and consequences of the Black Death in England up to the 1450s

Introduction

The Black Death is the term that has been commonly used since the eighteenth century to describe the virulent plague that spread across Asia and Europe in the 1340s. It arrived in England, at the port of Melcombe Regis in Dorset, in June 1348. By December 1349, it had spread across most of the British Isles. It is uncertain how many lives were lost to the Black Death in this period, but estimates suggest a dramatic decline in population from between 4 and 5 million to around 3 million. The population continued to decline, though less dramatically, for many years after 1349; recovery to the pre-1348 figure for population would not be achieved until well into the sixteenth century.

Historians believe the social, economic and political consequences of the Black Death were enormous. It is regarded as a major factor in the demise of medieval **feudalism** and its eventual replacement with a capitalist economic system. The Peasants' Revolt of 1381, considered by some as the most important popular rebellion in the history of England, can be traced to the Black Death and the attempts of the Crown to undermine the opportunity of wage-earners to exploit the shortage of labourers in the agrarian economy. A strong case has been made for the claim that workers were relatively well off in the fifteenth century due to the continuing shortage of labour.

Outbreaks of the plague in England occurred with some regularity before its decline in the middle of the sixteenth century.

The following sources highlight the impact and consequences of the Black Death.

> **Feudalism**
>
> The political and economic system of the medieval period by which land was held in return for services to a lord.

> ### Source 9 Extracts from the chronicle of an eyewitness
>
> *In this same year [1348] a great number of sheep died throughout the whole country, so much so that in one field alone more than five thousand sheep were slain. Their bodies were so corrupted by the plague that neither beast nor bird would touch them. The price of every commodity fell heavily since, because of their fear of death, men seemed to have lost their interest in wealth or in worldly goods… Sheep and cattle were left to wander through the fields and among the standing crops since there was no one to drive them off or collect them; for want of people to look after them they died in untold numbers in the hedgerows and ditches all over the country. So few servants and labourers were left that nobody knew where to turn for help.*
>
> *… The workers were so elated and uncooperative they did not heed the orders of the king prohibiting higher wages. If anyone wanted to hire them, they had to give them what they desired…*
>
> From the chronicle of Henry Knighton, canon of Leicester Abbey, around 1382

EXAM TIP

Although Knighton lived through the events he describes, you should note that his account was written several decades later.

Knighton's account in source 9 dates from around the time of the Peasants' Revolt of 1381 and the chronicler could be making a connection between the effects of the Black Death and subsequent rebellion.

> ### Source 10 Estimated daily payments (excluding remuneration in non-cash payments) for English agricultural workers, 1348–50
>
> | | 1348 | 1349 | 1350 |
> |---|---|---|---|
> | Thresher per day | 2½d | 6d | 4½d |
> | Mower per day | 5d | 9d | 9d |
> | Ploughman per annum | 2s | 7s | 10s 6d |
>
> Conversion to modern currency values: 6d (pence) = 2.5p; 1s (shilling) = 5p

Source 10 sheds some light on the short-term Impact of the Black Death.

What broad conclusions can be drawn from this evidence?

What are the limitations of this evidence for understanding the consequences of the Black Death?

Source 11 — Record of appointment of clergy as rectors or vicars of parishes in which the former incumbent, typically, had died

Dorset (previous average: one institution per month)

Year	Month	Number of institutions
1348	October	4
1348	November	17
1348	December	28
1349	January	21
1349	February	12
1349	March	12
1349	April	6
1349	May	9
1349	June	3
1349	July	11
1349	August	5

Somerset (previous average: nine institutions per month)

Year	Month	Number of institutions
1348	November	9
1348	December	32
1348	January	47
1349	February	43
1349	March	36
1349	April	40
1349	May	21
1349	June	7

Berkshire

Year	Number of institutions
1345	30
1346	56
1347	54
1348	190
1349	145
1350	93
1351	66

J. H. Bettey (1986) *Wessex from AD 1000*, Longman, pp. 86–88.

Source 12 — The medieval obsession with death?

'The legend of the three living and the three dead' by the Italian artist, Bernardo Daddi (1290–1348), an Italian altarpiece, is thought to have been painted between 1327 and 1348

The paintings above show a popular subject for medieval artists until the Renaissance: The morality tale of the three living and the three dead. Such paintings have sometimes been taken as evidence of the morbid obsessions of Europeans in the wake of the Black Death. The painting on the right reveals three cadavers. A monk is reminding the three princes (the horseman in the left-hand painting) of their fate: 'As you are, we were once. As we are, you will be.'

Source 13 The Black Death in Dorset

The mortality of men in the present pestilence is so great that the lands thereof be untilled and the profits are lost.

From the accounts of the estates held by the Crown around Bere Regis and Charminster for July 1349

Source 14 Contemporary claims regarding mortality figures and the consequences of the Black Death

To our great grief, the plague carried off so vast a multitude of people of both sexes that nobody could be found who would bear the corpses to the grave. Men and women carried their own children on their shoulders to the church and threw them into a common pit... There was so marked a deficiency of labourers and workmen of every kind that more than a third of the land in the whole realm was let lie idle. All the labourers, skilled or unskilled, were so carried away by the spirit of revolt that neither King, nor law, nor justice, could restrain them.

From the chronicle of William of Dene, a monk who lived in Kent

Source 15 The Black Death in Somerset

*The contagious pestilence of the present day, which is spreading far and wide, has left many parish churches and other livings in our diocese without parson or priest to care for their parishioners. Since no priests can be found who are willing, whether out of zeal and devotion or in exchange for a **stipend**, to take on the pastoral care of these aforesaid places, nor to visit the sick and administer to them the Sacraments of the Church (perhaps for fear of infection and contagion), we understand that many people are dying without the Sacrament of the Penance...*

From a letter from the Bishop of Bath and Wells to the priests in his diocese, January 1349

Stipend

A wage or salary.

To what extent do sources 13, 14 and 15 substantiate the evidence of source 11?

Source 16 The conclusion of a modern historian regarding the impact of the Black Death

Its [the Black Death's] impact should not be underestimated with a third to a half of the population killed, but it was for many the final blow that served to accelerate a decline which had its origins generations earlier. Its endemic nature meant that the disease continued to affect the population for centuries thereafter. The outbreaks of plague in 1361 and 1381, for example, were equally serious as that of 1348.

L. Viner (2002) *Lost Villages*, Dovecote Press, pp. 30–31.

How has the historian in source 16 revised the traditional view of the impact of the impact of the Black Death?

What evidence would you need to verify her claims?

THINK LIKE AN HISTORIAN

Now consider sources 9–16 as a set and work through the following exercises to test the validity of this interpretation:

The Black Death of 1348–49 caused social and economic disaster for the people of fourteenth-century England.

1. Explain how far the sources support this interpretation. You may, if you wish, amend the interpretation or suggest a different interpretation. If you do this, you must use the sources to support the changes you make.

EXAM TIP

Remember not to simply take the sources at face value. Use your knowledge of the period to interpret and evaluate them.

2. Explain how these sources are both useful and raise problems and issues for an historian using them.

EXAM TIP

Before submitting your answer to the questions above and moving on to the next case study, use the key areas checklist on page 72 to make sure you have taken the right approach for a top grade.

Case study 3: Protest and rebellion in Tudor England, 1489–1601

Introduction

The Tudor period began with the reign of Henry VII in 1485 and ended with the death of Elizabeth I in 1603. During this time, Tudor governments had to deal with a number of major rebellions, caused by a variety of political, economic and social factors. In some cases, rebellions appear to have had a single major cause, but in others the explanation for why so many people should rebel in a particular area at a particular point in time is much more complicated.

The sources that follow focus on the causes of rebellion in Tudor England. In an epoch, which is perhaps most clearly defined by the shift from the medieval Catholic form of worship to the Protestant Church of England, it is reasonable to hypothesise that religion in the history of Tudor rebellions was a significant factor. A careful study of the contemporary sources will help us to evaluate the validity of the argument that religion was a, perhaps the, major cause of rebellion in the Tudor period.

- **1489:** a rebellion in Yorkshire
- **1497:** the Cornish rebellion
- **1525:** the 'Amicable Grant' rebellion
- **1536:** the Lincolnshire rising
- **1549:** the Western (i.e. Cornwall and Devon) rebellion
- **1549:** Kett's Rebellion
- **1554:** Wyatt's rebellion
- **1569:** the rebellion of the Northern Earls
- **1601:** the rebellion of the Earl of Essex

▌ Figure 4.1 Major rebellions of the Tudor period.

Source (17)   A Tudor account of the Amicable Grant rebellion of 1525

... Now were commissioners sent to the clergy for the fourth part of their land and moveables; and in every assembly the priests answered that they would pay nothing...

*When this matter was opened throughout England ... all people cursed the cardinal [**Wolsey**] and his co-adherents, as subversor of the laws and liberty of England. For they said, if men should give their goods by a commission ... England should be bond and not free.*

From Edward Hall's 'Chronicle'

QUICK FACT

Cardinal Wolsey was Henry VIII's lord chancellor and, in 1525, he was held personally responsible for the introduction of the Amicable Grant, a tax that was imposed without parliamentary sanction.

Sources 18, 20 and 21 are all extracts from lists of demands, manifestos, made by Tudor rebels. In an age when most people were illiterate, this implies that the people who wrote the manifestos and, very likely, the people who drew them up in the first place, were members of a literate elite. Their particular interests, therefore, were not necessarily the same as those they led into rebellion. Furthermore, manifestos can be considered a form of propaganda which might intentionally exaggerate some issues while playing down others. Consequently, sources of this nature need to be handled with caution.

Source (18)   A selection from the demands of supporters of the Pilgrimage of Grace in 1536

1.   *... the heresies ... within this realm to be annulled and destroyed.*
2.   *... to have the supreme head of the church ... restored unto the see of Rome as before it was accustomed to be...*
3.   *... that the Lady Mary be made legitimate and the former statute therein annulled...*
4.   *To have the abbeys suppressed to be restored unto their houses, land and goods.*
6.   *To have the Observant Friars restored to their houses again.*
7.   *To have the heretics ... [punished] by fire...*
8.   *To have the lord Cromwell, the Lord Chancellor, and Sir Richard Riche ... to be punished as the subvertors of the good laws of this realm and maintainers of ... heretics...*
10.   *The statutes of handguns and crossbows to be repelled ... unless it be in the King's Forest or parks for the killing of his grace's deer...*
13.   *Statute for [the reversal of recent] enclosures ... to be put into execution...*
15.   *To have the parliament shortly summoned in a convenient place such as Nottingham or York.*
22.   *That the common laws may have place as was used in the beginning of your grace's reign...*

From 'Copy of the articles to the Lords of the King's
Council at our coming to Pontefract', December 1536

1. Why, according to source 17, did so many ordinary people in England rebel in 1525?

2. Edward Hall numbers priests among the rebels. Does this mean the Amicable Grant rebellion was religiously motivated?

3. How similar in terms of causation was this rebellion to the two major rebellions that preceded it?

Source 19 'The five wounds of Christ'

'The five wounds of Christ', an image of Jesus showing him bleeding from each of the wounds caused by his crucifixtion, became the badge of the Pilgrims of Grace, sown on to their clothes and banners. It is part of the propaganda of a popular movement that was unprecedented in its organisation and self-promotion

What image of the rebels and their purpose was the badge of the five wounds designed to promote? How far can such propaganda be accepted at face value in the search for the motives of Tudor rebels?

How does this emblem compare with the badges of modern protest movements?

QUICK FACT

The Six Articles – this act of 1539 preserved key Catholic traditions in the English Church, including the central place of the Mass in services.

Source 20 A selection from the demands of the Western rebels, 1549

1 *First we will have the general counsel and holy decree of our forefathers observed, kept and performed, and who so ever shall speak against them, we hold them as heretics.*

2 *We will have the Laws of our Sovereign Lord King Henry the VIII concerning* **the Six Articles,** *to be used as they were in his time.*

3 *We will have the mass in Latin, as was before, and celebrated by the priest without any man or woman, communicating with him.*

4 *We will have the Sacrament hung over the high altar, and there to be worshipped as it used to be, and they which will not thereunto consent, we will have them die like heretics against the holy Catholic faith.*

7 *We will have holy bread and holy water made every Sunday, palms and ashes at the time accustomed, images to be set up again in every church, and all other ancient old Ceremonies used as heretofore, by our mother the holy church.*

8 *We will not receive the new service because it is but like a Christmas game. We will have our old service of matins, Mass and evensong and procession as it was before; and we utterly refuse the new English.*

9 *We will have every preacher in his sermon, and every priest at the Mass pray, especially by name, for the souls in purgatory as our forefathers did.*

10 *We will have the whole Bible and all books of scripture in English to be called in again…*

Selected from a total of 16 articles

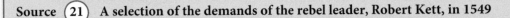

Source 21   A selection of the demands of the rebel leader, Robert Kett, in 1549

1   *We pray your grace that where it is enacted for enclosing that it be not hurtful…*

3   *We pray your grace that no lord of no manor shall common upon the Commons.*

7   *We pray that all Bushels within your realm be of one size, that is to say, to be in measure viii gallons.*

8   *We pray that priests or vicars that be not able to preach and set forth the word of God to his parishioners may be thereby put from his benefice, and the parishioners there to choose another or else the patron or lord of the town.*

10   *We pray that no man under the degree of a knight or a squire keep a dove house, except that it has been an old and ancient custom.*

11   *We pray that all freeholders and copyholders may take the profits of all commons, and there to common, and the lords not to common nor take profits from the same.*

15   *We pray that no priest shall be a chaplain… [unless he be] resident upon [his] benefice whereby [his] parishioners may be entrusted with the laws of God.*

20   *We pray that every … parson or vicar having a benefice … shall either by themselves or by some other person teach poor men's children of the parish the book called the Catechism and the Primer…*

From 'Kett's Demands being in Rebellion', 1549

Source 22   Instructions issued by the Crown in 1548 to commissioners investigating the problem of enclosures

… ye shall enquire what towns, villages, and hamlets have been decayed and, laid down by enclosures … what lands were then in tillage at the time of the said enclosure and what then in pasture … how many ploughs by reason of the said enclosure be laid down … [How many] cottages, and dwelling houses are decayed and inhabitation gone, and what lands they had … By whom, and when and how, were the enclosures made … Who has the inheritance and profits and of whom are they held … How many parks have been made since the said time … What 'arable' land has been thus imparked … How many ploughs, houses and inhabitations are thereby decayed … Who keeps above 2000 sheep besides lambs of one year's age, and whether upon own or his farm lands or otherwise by … fraud and how long he hath kept them … How many sheep you think necessary for such persons' households … If any person has occupied more than two houses or tenements of husbandry in one town, village, hamlet, or tithing.

From the Commission of Inquiry concerning Enclosures, 1 June 1548

Source 23   Mary I's opinion regarding the causes of Wyatt's rebellion

*I am come to you in mine own person to tell you that which already you see and know; that is how traitorously and rebelliously a number of Kentish men have assembled themselves against both us and you. Their pretence (as they said at the first) was for a marriage determined for us; to the which end to all the articles thereof ye have been made privy. But since, we have caused certain of our **Privy Council** to go again unto them … and it appeared then unto our said Council that the matter of the marriage seemed to be but a Spanish cloak to cover their pretended purpose against our religion…*

From Mary I's speech at the Guildhall, London, January 1554

1. Which of the statements in the three manifestos are concerned with religion? What does this seem to reveal regarding the main cause of each of these rebellions?

2. Does it matter that the manifestos have not been presented here in their entirety? If so, why?

3. It has been suggested that political faction fighting was a causal factor of rebellion in 1536. Which clause in source 18 supports this argument?

4. How far do you think the manifestos of the leaders can provide a complete picture of the reasons why thousands of ordinary people on occasions like these supported the rebellions they helped to coordinate?

5. To what extent were the leaders of rebellions likely to be completely honest regarding their intentions when writing their manifestos?

How can source 22 be used to support a hypothesis regarding the cause of any one of the rebellions mentioned in sources 18 to 21?

According to Mary I, in source 23, the declaration of the rebels regarding their reason for rebelling in 1554 was a 'pretence'.

What was the 'pretended' reason? What was the 'real' reason?

Whom should we believe – Queen Mary or the rebels from Kent – and why?

QUICK FACT

The **Privy Council** is the forerunner of the modern prime minister's Cabinet.

1. What reason for their rebellion, in addition to religion, do the Northern rebels give in source 24 to justify their actions?

2. How might this second reason have helped their cause?

3. Should we believe what they said in this instance?
   Give reasons to justify your opinion.

Source ㉔ Reasons given by the Northern Earls for their rebellion in 1569

Whereas diverse newly set up nobles about the Queen Majesty, have and do daily not only go about to overthrow and put down the ancient nobility of this realm, but also have misused the Queen Majesty's own person, and also have by the space of twelve years now past, set up, and maintained a newfound religion and heresy, contrary to God's word. For the amending and redressing thereof, diverse foreign powers do purpose shortly to invade this realm, which will be to our utter destruction, if we do not ourselves speedily forfend the same.

From the Proclamation of the Earls, 1569

Source ㉕ A modern historian summarises the principle causes of Tudor rebellions

What then were the patterns and themes of the rebellions of the sixteenth century? They … were essentially movements of peaceful resistance to specific government policies.

Only one clear theme of national significance ran through the rebellions. This was the opposition of a conservative and pious society to the English Reformation … the Church was in danger, rituals and customs which were known and treasured because they had become habitual were being abolished. The growth of English Protestantism was a long and tortuous process and little was done in the Tudor period to teach the new faith in the counties furthest from London. The religious motives of Tudor rebels were motives of uncertainty and bewildered insecurity. The rebels were parochial because local chantries, shrines and monasteries were of more significance to them than new statements of faith from London. In most cases they tried to besiege the provincial capital, for example Exeter, Carlisle or Norwich. And their agrarian grievances took their distinctive form from the character of particular farming regions.

Tudor Rebellions then were essentially the responses of local communities to local grievances.

A. Fletcher (1983) *Tudor Rebellions*, Longman, p.101.

How far is source 25 more 'reliable' than the previous six? Does this make it more 'useful'?

THINK LIKE AN HISTORIAN

Now consider sources 17–25 as a set and work through the following activities to test the validity of this interpretation:
Religion was the most significant cause of rebellion in the Tudor period.

1. Explain how far the sources support this interpretation. You may, if you wish, amend the interpretation or suggest a different interpretation. If you do this, you must use the sources to support the changes you make.

EXAM TIP

Remember not to simply take the sources at face value. Use your knowledge of the period to interpret and evaluate them.

2. Explain how these sources are both useful and raise problems and issues for an historian using them.

EXAM TIP

Before submitting your answer to the questions above and moving on to the next case study, use the key areas checklist on page 72 to make sure you have taken the right approach for a top grade.

Case study 4: Radicalism, popular politics and control, 1780s–1880s

Introduction

The history of western Europe from the 1780s to the 1880s can be described as an age of revolutions. France experienced violent political revolutions in 1789, 1830, 1848 and 1871. Much of Europe saw revolutions in 1848–49. During the same period, major popular protests occurred in Britain and reforms that permanently changed the social and political face of Britain were enacted through parliament. However, these changes were achieved without the dramatic overthrow of the existing system. It would appear likely that the willingness of regimes to reform themselves and the moderate views of the radicals that campaigned for change combined to prevent the bloody revolutions experienced elsewhere. A careful analysis of contemporary sources can shed some light on the degree to which Britain ever came close to revolution in this period.

The first major disturbances of the nineteenth century concerned machine breaking. Although not confined exclusively to the north, the destruction of the machines that threatened skilled, well-paid handcraft workers in the woollen cloth industry peaked in Nottinghamshire and Yorkshire in 1812. Mills were attacked at night by armed gangs, thousands of soldiers were sent into the troubled areas to suppress the troubles, one mill owner was ambushed and shot dead and three men were subsequently hanged for his murder. The situation was all the more alarming for a government reeling from the assassination of its prime minister, Spencer Perceval, in May 1812, shot by a bankrupt in the lobby of the House of Commons.

The machine-breakers in the north were known as Luddites after the name of their, probably, fictitious leader, Ned Ludd, a name conjured up by protestors to preserve their anonymity and to build up a Robin Hood style, hero-leader myth. Source 26 is one of many letters that have survived that is attributed to Ned Ludd.

Source 26 — The Luddites

Sir,

Information has just been given in, that you are the holder of those detestable Shearing Frames, and I was desired by men to write to you, and give you fair warning to pull them down, ... that if they are not taken down, I shall detach one of my lieutenants with at least three hundred men to destroy them, ... and if you have the impudence to fire at any of my men, they have orders to murder you and burn all your Housing ... by the last returns there were 2782 sworn heroes bound in a bone of necessity, either to redress their grievances or perish in the attempt, in the army of Huddersfield alone, nearly double sworn men in Leeds ... the weavers in Glasgow will join us ... the Papists in Ireland are rising to a man ... the immediate cause of this beginning was that rascally letter of the Prince Regent to the Lords Grey and Grenville which left us no hope for a change for the better ... but we hope with the assistance of the French Emperor is shaking off the yoke of the Rottonest, wickedest and most Tyrannical Government that ever existed ... and we will be governed by a just Republic ... we will never lay down our arms till the House of Commons passes an act to put down all machinery hurtful to the Commonality and repeal that to the Frame Breakers – but we petition no more, that won't do, fighting must.

Signed by the General of the Army of Redressers.

Ned Ludd

Clerk

From a letter to the master of a mill in Yorkshire, 1812

Consider the purpose of the letter in source 26.

How far can it be relied upon to shed light on the revolutionary intent of the Luddite movement as a whole?

In the aftermath of the Napoleonic Wars, ending at the battle of Waterloo in 1815, agitation for political reform increased as people increasingly saw this as the path to the improvement of their economic condition. In striking contrast to the tactics of the Luddites, they resorted to peaceful demonstrations – mass meetings to pressurise governments into constitutional change. The reaction of government to such initiatives helps reveal the level of contemporary concern that the country could be on the brink of revolution. In 1819, a colossal meeting of between 50,000 and 200,000 people in Manchester at St Peter's Fields was broken up by the middle-class, part-time, local militia, the Yeomanry, resulting in eleven deaths and hundreds of people injured.

1. In source 27, where do the artist's sympathies seem to lie – with the yeomanry or the demonstrators?

2. How useful is this source as evidence for the potential for revolution in Britain in this period?

Source 27 The 'Peterloo Massacre', 1819

A contemporary depiction of the 'Peterloo Massacre' showing the radical orator, Henry Hunt (centre), banners supporting the values of the French Revolution, and the yeomanry breaking up the demonstration

Such draconian actions as the Peterloo Massacre failed to stifle demands for full democratic reforms, including the vote for all – universal suffrage. By 1831, political unions, organisations with memberships of tens of thousands, had sprung up in cities across Britain. When the House of Lords rejected a bill for parliamentary reform that had been passed by the Commons, rioting erupted in towns across the country. A figurehead of the movement, Thomas Attwood, a banker from Birmingham, used some strong rhetoric in a meeting of 200,000 in the city in May 1832 – see source 28.

Source 28 The Reform crisis, 1831–32

I would rather die than see the great Bill of reform rejected or mutilated. I see that you are all of one mind on the subject … Answer me then, had you rather not die than live slaves of the boroughmongers? (All! All!)

From a speech by Thomas Attwood, May 1832

On the face of it, this seems revolutionary, a battle cry for the masses in the struggle to overhaul the existing system. Should political speeches always be taken at face value? It has been argued that in this instance middle-class radicals like Attwood were engaged in a campaign to alarm the conservative lords into making moderate reforms that would benefit the middle - classes but not the working - class whose support they were courting.

In Source 29, a strong case is made for the argument that the middle-class reformers who promoted the Great Reform Bill which eventually won them the vote in 1832 were anything but revolutionary!

Source 29   The Great Reform Bill

*The Bill was never intended to do you one particle of good. The object of its promoters was not to change that 'glorious constitution', which has entailed upon you so much misery, but to make it immortal. They projected the Bill, not with a view to subvert, or even re-model our aristocratic institutions, but to consolidate them by a reinforcement of sub-aristocracy from the middle classes ... The **Whigs** have too much to lose to desire real reform ... they framed the BILL, in the hope of drawing to the feudal aristocrats and yeomanry of counties a large reinforcement of the middle class ... and make common cause with them in keeping down the people, and thereby to quell the rising spirit of democracy in England.*

From the *Poor Man's Guardian*, October 1832

Following the passing of the Reform Bill of 1832 fresh demands for the enfranchisement of working people were made and a new movement, **Chartism**, was born. All Chartists advocated universal suffrage, but they differed over the methods by which this would be achieved.

Source 30   Physical force Chartism

At least eight thousand men, mostly miners employed in the neighbourhood (which is very densely populated) were engaged in the attack upon the town of Newport and ... many of them were armed ... The ultimate design of the leaders does not appear; but it probably was to rear the standard of rebellion throughout Wales, in hopes of being able to hold the royal forces at bay, in that mountainous district, until the people of England, assured by successes, should rise en masse, for the same objects. According to the evidence now before the world, Mr Frost, the late member of the Convention, led the rioters, and he, with others, has been committed for high treason. On entering Newport, the people marched straight to the Westgate Hotel, where the magistrates, with about 40 soldiers were assembled, being fully apprised of the intended outbreak. The Riot Act was read, and the soldiers fired down, with ease and security, upon the people who had first broken and fired into the windows. About thirty of the people are known to have been killed, and several to have been wounded.

From a Chartist newspaper account of the Newport Rising, 3–4 November 1839

In the wake of another revolution in France in 1848, a mass Chartist demonstration was organised for 10 April. Its aim was to present Parliament with a petition bearing, allegedly, nearly six million genuine signatures. Queen Victoria left the mainland for the Isle of Wight and the authorities prepared for a violent uprising which never came; it rained and thousands of anticipated marchers failed to show. The petition for reform was submitted and rejected.

QUICK FACT

The **Whigs** was a nickname for the political grouping most associated with the passage of the major social and political reforms of the first half of nineteenth century. Their successors were the Liberal Party.

Source 29 is an extract from an article in a radical newspaper.

What was its target audience?

What was its purpose?

QUICK FACT

Chartism was named after the 'People's Charter', which was presented to Parliament and which contained their six demands. The movement existed to win the vote for the working class and reform the political system.

How far does source 30 support the notion that Chartism was a revolutionary movement?

The *Northern Star* was a Chartist newspaper.

Does this make its reporting of the events of 10 April in source 31 any more or less reliable?

Source 31 — Preparations for a Chartist uprising, London 1848

A breastwork of sandbags, with loopholes for muskets and small guns had been thrown up along the parapet wall of [the Bank of England], at each corner of the building, musket batteries, bullet proof, were raised, having loopholes for small carronades.

The line of the road from the Strand to the new Houses of Parliament has all the appearance of a thoroughfare in a besieged capital. Notices from the Police Commissioners, that no carts, vans or omnibuses are to be allowed upon the road from Abingdon street to Cockspur Street after eleven o'clock, and that no delay is to be permitted in the other streets, agitate the public, and the appearance of patrols of mounted police, and of single files of soldiers in the usually quiet street, is ominous and alarming.

From the *Northern Star*, 15 April 1848

The President and the Secretary of the Council of the People's Charter Union stated the official Chartist position a few days after the demonstration of 10 April.

Source 32 — Moral force Chartism

We disclaim all desire of injuring others, all sympathy with acts of outrage or disorder. We desire by peaceable and legal means, and by them alone, to alter and amend the institutions of the country: by establishing its legislative system upon the only true basis – the ascertained will of the majority, at once the guarantee of present order, and the promise of peaceful growth and happiness for the future.

From Address of the People's Charter Union, 17 April 1848

The year 1848 was the third and final time the Chartists petitioned parliament. The movement continued well into the 1850s, but it never regained its former popularity and dynamism.

1. What are the elements of a revolution scenario that Wright identified (see source 33)? Which of these is evident in sources 26–32?

2. What advantages does a modern observer like Wright have over contemporary observers when measuring, how close Britain came to revolution in this period?

Source 33 — A modern historian reviews the evidence for the possibility of a revolution occurring in the early 1830s

Without doubt, some of the ingredients of revolution were present. Among them were economic distress, unrest among both industrial and agricultural workers, the influence of the July Revolution in Paris and signs of a serious division among the ruling class. There was also a well organised radical movement, including organisations like the Birmingham Political Union, the National (i.e. London) Political Union and the National Union of the Working Classes. Neither can it be denied that widespread support existed in the country for the government and the Reform Bill… Moreover, the Reform crisis was regularly punctuated by violence… Non-political violence also aggravated feelings of insecurity at a time when the forces of public order were weak and memories of the French Revolution were strong. Important manifestations of this kind of violence were a renewed outbreak late in 1831 of the rural arson and machine breaking of late 1830 and violent strikes in the mining areas of Northumberland, Durham, Staffordshire and Wales. There is evidence of alarm among the ruling classes. J. C. Hobhouse, a radical MP and later a Whig minister, wrote in his 1832 diary that many of the aristocracy 'believe themselves, and perhaps are, on the brink of destruction'.

D. G. Wright (1970) *Democracy and Reform 1815–1885*, Longman, p. 41

Many historians have seen the crisis leading up to the 1832 Reform Act as the point at which Britain came closest to revolution in the first half of the nineteenth century. At this time, unlike in the later Chartist period, the middle class and the working class appeared to be united in their aim to overhaul the system. A counter-argument, however, is that the violent rhetoric of middle-class leaders like Attwood (see source 28) was designed merely to scare politicians into supporting reform. Arguably, without a middle-class leadership willing to engage in revolution, one could not have occurred in Britain in this period.

THINK LIKE AN HISTORIAN

Now consider sources 26–33 as a set and work through the following activities to test the validity of this interpretation:

Britain did not come close to revolution at any point during the first half of the nineteenth century.

1. Explain how far the sources support this interpretation. You may, if you wish, amend the interpretation or suggest a different interpretation. If you do this, you must use the sources to support the changes you make.

EXAM TIP

Remember not to simply take the sources at face value. Use your knowledge of the period to interpret and evaluate them.

2. Explain how these sources are both useful and raise problems and issues for an historian using them.

EXAM TIP

Before submitting your answer to the questions above and moving on to the next case study, use the key areas checklist on page 72 to make sure you have taken the right approach for a top grade.

Case study 5: European Nationalism, 1815–1914: Germany and Italy

Introduction

Nationalism

In the nineteenth century, the term nationalism defined the concept of economic and political unity for people of a recognisably unique nationality. This, in turn, was defined by a common language, common customs and traditions and, typically, clearly identifiable geographical boundaries separating one nation from another. The experience of conquest during the **French Revolutionary** and **Napoleonic Wars** helped to promote nationalism in Europe after 1815. Nationalists in Germany and Italy, which until towards the end of the century were broken up into many principalities, advocated the formation of a single **nation-state** that could aspire to the triumphs of the nation-states of France, Britain and Spain. National unity meant strength and the way forward for those that sought liberation from control by foreign powers. At the start of the nineteenth century, its advocates had liberal political objectives: the forming of parliamentary systems in place of despots and tyrants. The principle of democracy sat comfortably with that of nationalism and the forming nation-states in which the people who formed the nation were in control. By the end of the century,

QUICK FACT

French Revolutionary and **Napoleonic Wars**

– wars between Britain and France between 1793 and 1815.

Nation-state

A society organised around the concept of territory that is historically and culturally identified with a particular people.

however, as competition between nation-states developed and national minorities threatened revolution and the disintegration of empires, nationalism, especially in Germany, stood in the way of further democratisation. Where formerly nationalism was associated with the overthrow of tyrants and the dismantling of their empires, in Germany it had itself become a force of imperialistic aggrandisement and the warfare this entailed.

> 'The principle of all sovereignty resides essentially in the nation.'
>
> From *The Declaration of the Rights of Man*,1789, the most important statement of belief in the first phase of the French Revolution. It remained the philosophical keystone of European liberalism for the next half century.

Italy

After the failure of nationalist movements in the 1830s and 1840s, the unification of Italy, or **Risorgimento**, was achieved during the period 1850–70. By 1860, the northern states were united with the kingdom of Piedmont, Lombardy having been liberated from Austria after a short war. The kingdom of Italy was declared in 1861, the result of a combined, though unplanned, effort of Italian nationalists marching from Sicily in the south, led by Garibaldi, and the unified principalities of the north under the leadership of the Piedmontese prime minister, Cavour. After a war against Austria, Venetia was added in 1866. Finally Rome was incorporated in 1870. Further territories in the north around the Adriatic were annexed after the First World War.

Germany

After the failure of nationalist movements in the 1830s and 1840s, the unification of Germany was fashioned by the chief minister of Prussia, Otto von Bismarck. The German empire was proclaimed in 1871 following three wars: with Denmark in 1864, Austria in 1866 and France in 1870. As its first imperial chancellor, Bismarck resisted further expansion and German-speaking Austria retained its independence until the Anschluss of 1938 when it was annexed to Germany by Hitler. Bismarck fiercely opposed liberal politics and established an authoritarian, conservative unified state.

The following sources focus on the nature, causes and aims of nationalism in Italy and Germany in the nineteenth and early twentieth centuries.

Source 34 Italian unity

We are a people of from one-and-twenty to two-and-twenty millions of men, known from time immemorial by the same name, as the people of Italy; enclosed by natural limits the clearest ever marked out by the Deity – the sea and the highest mountains in Europe; speaking the same language, modified by dialects varying from each other less than do the Scotch and the English; having the same creeds, the same manners, the same habits ... proud of the noblest tradition in politics, science and art, that adorns European history; having twice given to Humanity a tie, a watchword of Unity-once, in the Rome of the Emperors, again, ere they had betrayed their mission, in the Rome of the Popes; gifted with active, ready and brilliant faculties ... rich in every source of material well-being that, fraternally and liberally worked, could make ourselves happy, and open to sister nations the brightest prospect in the world.

From the memoirs of Mazzini, 1845

Source (35) Italian disunity

We have no flag, no political name, no rank, among European nations. We have no common centre, no common fact, no common market. We are dismembered into eight States – Lombardy, Parma, Tuscany, Modena, Lucca, the Popedom, Piedmont, the kingdom of Naples – all independent of one another, without alliance, without unity of aim, without organised connexion between them. Eight lines of custom houses, without counting the impediments appertaining to the internal administration of each State, sever our material interests, oppose our advancement, and forbid us large manufactures, large commercial activity, and all those encouragements to our capabilities that a centre of impulse would afford. Prohibitions or enormous duties check the import and export of articles of the first necessity in each State of Italy. Territorial and industrial products abound in one province that are deficient in another; and we may not freely sell the superfluities or exchange among ourselves the necessities. Eight different systems of currency, of weights and measures, of civil, commercial and penal legislation, of administrative organisation, and of police restriction, divide us, and render us as much as possible strangers to each other. And all these States among which we are partitioned are ruled by despotic Governments, in whose working the country has no agency whatever. There exists not in any of these States, either liberty of the press, or of united action, or of speech, or of collective petition, or of the introduction of foreign books, or of education, or of anything. One of these States, comprising nearly a fourth of the Italian population, belongs to the foreigner – to Austria; the others, some from family ties, some from a conscious feebleness, tamely submit to her influence.

From the memoirs of Mazzini, 1845

> According to source 35, what were the objectives of Mazzini and other Italian nationalists at the start of the nineteenth century?

Source (36) 'Right leg in the boot at last'

This British cartoon about the unification of Italy, which appeared in Punch in November 1860, comments on the respective roles of Garibaldi (left) and Victor Emmanuel (right).

Garibaldi: 'If it won't go on, Sire, try a little more powder.'

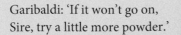

RIGHT LEG IN THE BOOT AT LAST.

GARIBALDI. "IF IT WON'T GO ON, SIRE, TRY A LITTLE MORE POWDER."

> Why would the British readership of the often cynical and sometimes satirical magazine Punch find this ironic cartoon serious as well as mildly amusing when it was published. What was the attitude in Britain to Italian unification?

Compare source 37 with sources 34 and 35 regarding the objectives of German and Italian nationalists at the beginning of the nineteenth century. Identify the points of similarity and points of difference.

Is there anything in source 39 that contradicts sources 34 and 35?

Compare source 38 with source 37. Consider to what extent, if at all, nationalism by the end of the nineteenth century continued to endorse the politics of liberalism.

According to source 39, what was the relationship between militaorism and nationalism in Germany?

Source 37 German nationalism

Our earliest common ancestors, the primordial stock of the new culture, the Germans, as the Romans called them, courageously resisted the world domination of the Romans.

… Our present problem … is simply to preserve the existence and continuity of what is German. All other differences vanish before this higher point of view … It is essential that the higher love of Fatherland, for the entire people of the German nation, reign supreme, and justly so, in every particular German state. No one of them can lose sight of the higher interest without alienating everything that is noble and good…

From Johann Gottlieb Fichte, 'Addresses to the German Nation', around 1808. (Fichte (1762–1814) was a German philosopher and founding figure of the philosophical approach known as German Idealism.)

Source 38 Kaiser Wilhelm II

Public opinion didn't concern him. He knew that people didn't love him, and cursed him; but that wouldn't deter him. I then reminded the Emperor of the difference between Prussia and the Empire; said that in Prussia he had old rights which continued to exist, so far as the Prussian Constitution had not limited them. In the Empire the Emperor had only the rights which the Reichstag [Germany's parliament] conceded to him. The Emperor interjected 'the Emperor hardly has any rights', which I attempted to refute. Besides, this was quite unimportant, said HM: the South German democratic states didn't worry him. He had 18 army corps and would make short work of the South Germans.

From a report by Prince Hohenlohe, a Bavarian politician, March 1897

Source 39 Government propaganda for the development of the German Navy

… the concept of the navy has indeed, as Prince Bismarck once said, been the hearth around which the German attempts at unity have clustered warmed themselves. Thus it has already helped to fulfil a great national mission. It has also, however, been allotted the further task of overcoming the discord between the parties in the united German Empire, and directing the minds of the disputants towards a higher goal: the greatness and glory of the Fatherland. Today millions of our compatriots are spiritually alienated from the state and the prevailing economic order; the concept of the navy possesses the power – that we have nowadays perceived – to revive the national spirit of the classes and fill them once again with patriotic loyalty and love for Kaiser and Reich.

From an official naval publication, *Nauticus*, 1900

Source (40) **War and nationalism, the official position of German Socialists regarding Germany's declaration of war on Russia, 1 August 1914**

We Social Democrats in this solemn hour are at one with the whole German nation, without distinction of party or creed, in accepting the fight forced upon us by Russian barbarism, and we are ready to fight till the last drop of blood for Germany's national independence, fame and greatness.

From *Der Volksfreund*, 1 August 1914

Source (41) **The conclusions of a modern historian**

*Nationalism and liberalism came into conflict with each other, and liberalism was to be the loser. This was foreshadowed in the events of the **revolutions of 1848**, when the revolutionaries revealed themselves unwilling to consider the rights of other peoples when they came into conflict with their own national aspirations. This was particularly true in the multi racial Austrian Empire, where the insurgents in Vienna gave neither sympathy nor support to the Italians… A similar attitude was adopted by the German liberals in that year, and their failure was held to indicate that a national state would only be established by organised military force; and in the following years German nationalism parted company with liberalism and became anti-democratic and warlike. Nor did international events indicate that the fulfilment of nationalist aims would bring any improvement in diplomatic relations and lead to co-operation between the countries of Europe.*

L. W. Cowie and R. Wolfson (1985) *Years of Nationalism*, Hodder & Stoughton, p. 383.

THINK LIKE AN HISTORIAN

Now consider sources 34–41 as a set and work through the following activities to test the validity of this interpretation:
Nineteenth- and early twentieth-century nationalism was primarily concerned with strength and unity, not freedom.

1. Explain how far the sources support this interpretation. You may, if you wish, amend the interpretation or suggest a different interpretation. If you do this, you must use the sources to support the changes you make.

EXAM TIP

Remember not to simply take the sources at face value. Use your knowledge of the period to interpret and evaluate them.

2. Explain how these sources are both useful and raise problems and issues for an historian using them.

EXAM TIP

Before submitting your answer to the questions above and moving on to the next case study, use the key areas checklist on page 72 to make sure you have taken the right approach for a top grade.

To what extent does source 40 substantiate the claims of source 39?

QUICK FACT

The **revolutions of 1848** took place in Italy, Germany, Austria, Hungary, Bohemia and France. They occurred for a variety of economic and political reasons, including support for liberal and nationalist ideas.

Summarise the observations of the modern historians quoted in source 41.

With full reference to sources 34–35 show how the claims of source 41 can be substantiated by primary sources.

Case study 6: Race and American society, 1865–1970s

Introduction

Central to the study of race and American society in modern times is the history of the civil rights movement. This term defines the struggle to give black Americans the vote and to end **segregation** in the south. The first major triumph was the Supreme Court decision outlawing segregation in schools in the Brown versus the Board of Education case of 1954. In 1955, in Montgomery, Alabama, Rosa Parks refused to change seats on a bus because of a city ruling that forbade black passengers sitting in the same section as white passengers. Her action and subsequent arrest prompted a boycott of buses to draw attention to discrimination while at the same time undermining the business interests of white-owned bus companies. Subsequently, two acts (1957 and 1960), passed under the Eisenhower administration, established an agency to investigate claims of racial discrimination regarding the issue of equal protection of the laws.

In the early 1960s, activists employed various forms of direct action such as 'sit-ins' at such places as cinemas, libraries and lunch-counters to speed up the process of desegregation. In August 1963, leading black activist Martin Luther King led 200,000 'Freedom Marchers' to Washington DC. Racial discrimination in areas such as education, employment and politics became illegal with the Civil Rights Act (1964) and the Voting Rights Act (1965) under the Johnson Administration. Although on a personal level, President Johnson shared the racist convictions common among white Americans at that time, he became publicly committed to desegregation in his pursuit of what he termed his 'Great Society'. The civil rights movement split in the late 1960s with the growth of a more radical and militant wing. In April 1968, Martin Luther King was assassinated.

> **QUICK FACT**
>
> From 1876, the 'Jim Crow laws' in the southern states of the USA legalised **segregation** of blacks and whites. Segregation extended to housing, school and public facilities. The laws kept whites and blacks separate on trains and buses, in schools, parks, theatres, restaurants and even in cemeteries.

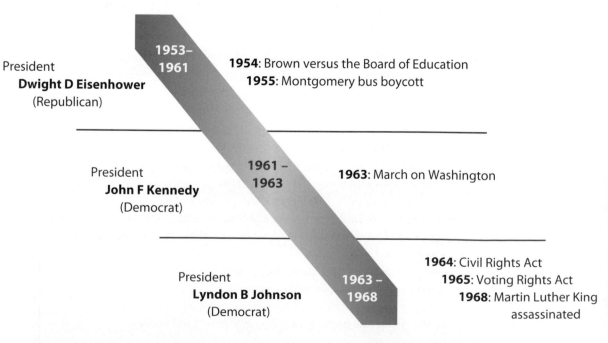

Figure 4.3

Landmark events in the campaign after the Second World World War for civil rights in America

The following sources have been selected to shed light on the forces of change regarding civil rights in the USA in the 1950s and 1960s.

> ### Source (42) Support for desegregation in the Supreme Court
>
> *We come then to the question presented: Does segregation of children in public schools solely on the basis of race, even though the physical facilities and other 'tangible' factors may be equal, deprive the children of the minority group of equal educational opportunities? We believe that it does.*
>
> Ruling of the US Supreme Court in Brown versus the Board of Education case (1954)

QUICK FACT

The **National Association for the Advancement of Colored People (NAACP)** was established in 1909 with a committee initially dominated by whites.

As mentioned in the introduction, the verdict of the Supreme Court in this case had a major impact. It concerned Oliver Brown's right to send his black daughter to an all-white school in the state of Kansas. In his appeal, he received the support of the **NAACP** and its leading lawyer. The Supreme Court agreed that the principle of segregated education contravened the **Fourteenth Amendment** and found in Brown's favour. President Eisenhower, however, refused to enforce the decision until rioters challenging the desegregation of schooling in Little Rock, Arkansas, in 1957, obliged him to send in federal troops and uphold the law in line with the findings of the Supreme Court.

Source 42 highlights the complexity of the issue. Progress in this instance was made through:

- the actions of individuals such as Brown and black students defying segregation in Little Rock by bravely entering white schools

- organisations and institutions, including the NAACP and the Supreme Court

- the various pressure groups on the ground forcing the government's hand through both passive resistance and riot.

QUICK FACT

The **Fourteenth Amendment** to the US Constitution, dating from 1868, was intended to secure rights for former slaves, and recognised their equal protection before the law.

> ### Source (43) Black resistance to discrimination
>
> *The Negro of 1956 who stands on his own two feet is not a new Negro; he is the grandson or the great grandson of the men who hated slavery. By his own hands, through his own struggles, in his own organised groups – of churches, fraternal societies, the NAACP and others – he has fought his way to the place where he now stands.*
>
> Roy Wilkins, black activist and leader of the NAACP, following the Montgomery bus boycott

Source 43 celebrates the role of black people in fighting for emancipation. The historian needs to consider how far black activism is the sole explanation for the recognition and enforcement of civil rights in the period.

> ### Source (44) Passive resistance and the work of the NAACP
>
> *I worked on numerous cases with the NAACP, but we did not get the publicity. There were cases of flogging, **peonage**, murder, and rape. We didn't seem to have too many successes. It was more a matter of trying to challenge the powers that be, and to let it be known that we did not wish to continue being second-class citizens.*
>
> From the recollections of Rosa Parks

Peonage

The practice of making a debtor work for their creditor until they had paid off the debt.

Compare sources 43 and 44. The latter could be considered more measured in its comments on the achievements of civil rights campaigners and their organisations.

Source 45   **The US president comments on the spirit of the age**

I hope that every American will stop and examine his conscience. Today we are committed to a worldwide struggle to promote and protect the rights of all who wish to be free. And when Americans are sent to Vietnam or West Berlin we do not ask for Whites only. Now the time has come for the nation to fulfil its promise. The fires of frustration and discord are burning in every city, north and south. We face therefore a moral crisis; it is time to act in Congress.

From a speech by President Kennedy, 1963

Kennedy's comments (source 45) place the American civil rights struggle in a worldwide context and introduce the notion that the answer to achievements in the US in this period might not be found in the history of that continent alone.

Source 46   **The Voting Rights Act, 1965**

Rarely are we met with a challenge … to the values and the purposes and the meaning of our beloved Nation. The issue of equal rights for American Negroes is such as an issue… the command of the Constitution is plain. It is wrong – deadly wrong – to deny any of your fellow Americans the right to vote in this country…The real hero of this struggle is the American Negro. His actions and protests, his courage to risk safety and even to risk his life, have awakened the conscience of this Nation…

From President Johnson's speech before Congress

Source 47   **Lyndon Johnson's fear of violence and civil disorder**

The Negro fought in the war, and … he's not gonna keep taking the shit we're dishing out. We're in a race with time. If we don't act, we're gonna have blood in the streets.

Comments of Lyndon Johnson when he was serving as vice-president to President John Kennedy

---

1. How might wars abroad have heightened demands for civil rights in the USA?

2. To what extent, according to the evidence of Source 45, was reform government driven?

In source 46, President Johnson gives full credit to black Americans for civil rights triumphs in the 1960s.

How far is this justified?

What precautions should historians take when considering the pronouncements of politicians as evidence?

Do Johnson's comments in source 47 sound like an official statement? Is it more or less reliable than source 46?

According to this source, which word best describes Johnson's outlook on the civil rights issue: creative or reactive?

Source 48   Civil rights

I hope that every American will stop and examine his conscience. Today we are committed to a worldwide struggle to promote and protect the rights of all who wish to be free. And when Americans are sent to Vietnam or West Berlin we do not ask for Whites only. Now the time has come for the nation to fulfil its promise. The fires of frustration and discord are burning in every city, north and south. We face therefore a moral crisis; it is time to act in Congress.

From a speech by President Kennedy, 1963

Anti-discrimination march in Cleveland, Ohio, early 1960s

Which of sources 42–48 could be used to substantiate the claim in Source 49?

Is the verdict of a modern historian likely to be more reliable than that of a contemporary witness?

Source 48 reinforces the claims of some of the other sources. Note the ethnic diversity of the civil rights campaigners in the photo.

Source 49   A historian's verdict on the role of President Johnson in the civil rights struggle

African Americans were the principal architects of their own success.

Robert Cook (1998) *Sweet Land of Liberty*, quoted in V. Saunders (2006) *Race Relations in the USA*, Hodder Murray, p. 191

THINK LIKE AN HISTORIAN

Now consider sources 42–49 as a set and work through the following activities to test the validity of this interpretation: Black activism was the main reason for the successes of the US civil rights movement in the 1950s and 1960s.

1. Explain how far the sources support this interpretation. You may, if you wish, amend the interpretation or suggest a different interpretation. If you do this, you must use the sources to support the changes you make.

EXAM TIP

Remember not to simply take the sources at face value. Use your knowledge of the period to interpret and evaluate them.

2. Explain how these sources are both useful and raise problems and issues for an historian using them.

EXAM TIP

Before submitting your answer to the questions above, use the key areas checklist on page 72 to make sure you have taken the right approach for a top grade.

ExamCafé

Relax, refresh, result!

RADICALISM, POPULAR POLITICS AND CONTROL, 1780s–1880s

Relax and prepare

Hot tips

What I wish I had known at the start of the year…

Susie

I wish I'd listened to my teacher from the beginning of the course when she said how important it was to work regularly – with plenty of reading and note-making. Before I knew it, the exams were just around the corner. My work was so rushed, I went into the exam knowing my result would be disappointing.

Wayne

It took me too long to realise what my teacher meant when he said not to make general comments about bias. Now I make sure I make comments about reliability and usefulness that are specific to the actual sources, based on the information given about each source on the exam paper – and my marks HAVE improved! At GCSE I never realised that a biased source is useful.

Nadine

My biggest problem was forgetting to add DETAILED knowledge to my answers, even though I was good at evaluating the sources. At first, I just tended to explain what they said, but now I know I just need to add some specific bits of own knowledge to support or challenge what the sources say – that gets me much better marks.

Refresh your memory

Key areas of knowledge for this topic are:

▷ **Britain in the 1780s.** You should be aware of the social and economic aspects of Britain in the 1780s, especially the changes in agriculture and industry and how these affected the living standards of the middle classes, artisans and labourers.

▷ **The form of government.** In particular, you will need to know about the very restricted franchise and William Pitt, who came to power in 1784 and remained head of the government for most of the time until his death in 1806. You will also need to be aware of the reforms many wanted to see.

▷ **Reactions to the French Revolution.** For instance, how Burke and Fox reacted in opposing ways; Tom Paine's initial support and reactions to his *Rights of Man* (1791); and the revival of British reform movements, such as the London Corresponding Society and the Whig Friends of the People. Also, remember the anti-radical groups, such as the Association for the Protection of Property against Republicans and Levellers.

▷ **The government response.** In particular, the various acts which attempted to restrict the activities of radicals, such as the Proclamation against Wicked and Seditious Writings of 1792, the suspension of Habeas Corpus in 1794 and the Seditious Meetings and Treason Acts of 1795.

Common mistakes

Joel

When considering the problems presented by particular sources – such as typicality, limitations regarding different viewpoints being presented – I never tried to suggest how these might be overcome or resolved. I now try to remember to do this where appropriate with specific recommendations, based on my own knowledge, NOT just general comments such as 'More sources needed'.

Examiner's tip

Remember to refer all the sources, and make explicit attempts to link or compare. You can do this by:

1. grouping the sources according to points on which they agree and points on which they do not, and

2. adding some own knowledge to confirm or challenge all the interpretations the sources give.

Get the result!

Exam question

The impact of the French Revolution in Britain

Read the interpretation and sources 1–5.

Interpretation:
Supporters of the French Revolution posed no serious threat to the established order in Britain during 1792–95.

(a) Explain how far sources 1–5 support this interpretation. You may, if you wish, amend the interpretation or suggest a different interpretation. If you do this, you must use the sources to support the changes you make. [35]

(b) Explain how these sources are both useful and raise problems and issues for a historian using them. [15]

Source 1

These historians comment on the membership of the London Corresponding Society:

'[What particularly alarmed the government was] the London Corresponding Society, with its much bigger membership, its weekly subscription of one penny, and its meetings in taverns or coffee houses. Its membership varied sharply from time to time: it was at one time put as high as ten thousand. This was probably an exaggeration, but it is fairly safe to assume that in 1792, '93 and '94 its membership was over three thousand, after the initial few weeks of its existence. (It was constituted on 25 January 1792.) The subscription was 1d a week and its membership was overwhelmingly working class – artisan or small tradesman.'

G. D. H. Cole and R. Postgate (1966) *The Common People, 1746–1946*, Methuen, pp.152 – 53.

Source 2

A government view of Tom Paine's *Rights of Man*, set out in the 'King's Proclamation against Wicked and Seditious Writings', 21 May 1792:

'We cannot see without indignation, the attempts which have been made to weaken in the minds of his majesty's subjects, sentiments of obedience … and attachment to the form of government.'

Cobbett's *Parliamentary History of England*, xxix (1791–92).

Source 3

This historian stresses that English supporters of the French Revolution did not pose a serious danger:

'In terms of membership, the Corresponding Societies never offered a real threat. The LCS at its peak in 1795 numbered about 5000; provincial radical societies were all smaller and some, for all their pernickety constitutions and their elaborate ground rules for orderly conduct of debate, had memberships in the dozens. Such calculations, however, miss the point. As with nonconformist sects, adherents and sympathizers were far more numerous than formal members and the societies could stage impressive displays of support in the open-air protest meetings which were such a feature between 1793 and 1795.'

E. Evans (1996) *The Forging of the Modern State: Early Industrial Britain 1783–1870*, Longman, pp.72 – 73.

Source 4

This biographer of Tom Paine stresses Pitt's fears about the political situation in 1792:

'Such talk [influenced by the *Rights of Man*] frightened the government of William Pitt, forcing it to face up to three related trends. First, the growing radicalisation of the French Revolution … Second, and closely related, the expansionist fervour of the French regime … Finally, in England, Wales, Scotland, and Ireland, there were growing signs of cooperation between extraparliamentary radicalism and the revolutionary forces in France. No great leap of imagination was needed to see that these three overlapping trends were revolutionary. That is why, during the course of 1792, the Pitt regime decided that the situation constituted an emergency and that it should act, if necessary using the armed forces of the state, to root out the Paineite disease.'

J. Keane (1995) *Tom Paine: A Political Life*, Bloomsbury, p.334.

Source 5

An extract from 'John Bull to His Brethren', a government-sponsored poster of 1792:

'Shall we trust to TOM the STAYMAKER, and his bungling French journeymen, to amend our Constitution?… Shall we commit our Property, Liberties, and Religion, to those who have robbed their own Church, murdered their Clergy, and denied their God?'

Cobbett-Bonneville Manuscripts, 451.

Susie's answer: question (a)

Overall, though these sources give both sides of the argument, they do not support the interpretation. The majority (sources 1, 2, 4 and 5) seem to suggest that the supporters of the French Revolution were a serious threat; while source 3 says otherwise. However, several of the sources also contain information which could be used to show the opposite of what they seem to be saying.

Sources 1 and 3 mainly focus on the membership of groups which supported the French Revolution. Both agree that their numbers were probably about 3000–5000 during the period 1792–5. Apart from the LCS, there were several other groups – such as the Friends of the People and the Society for Constitutional Information; like the LCS, these were all based in London. And, as source 3 says, there were other groups outside of London. However, the fact that they existed doesn't mean they were necessarily a serious threat – even though source 3 points out that their influence was greater than their membership numbers, the historian seems to conclude they were not a serious threat. Also, although source 1 says the LRC was 'alarming', it was written in 1966, 30 years before source 3, so it may be that source 3 has had access to more recent research. So, overall, these two sources could be taken as agreeing with the interpretation – or at least not convincingly disagreeing.

Sources 2 and 5 are primary sources, and seem to suggest more strongly they were a serious threat – 'Tom the Staymaker' (source 5) is Tom Paine, who was from Thetford in Norfolk where his father was a staymaker, and Tom Paine was also a staymaker for a time himself. In particular, why would the government issue proclamations and posters against the writings of Tom Paine if they were not seen as a serious threat, influencing large numbers of people? Tom Paine was a supporter of the French Revolution in its early phase (hence the reference to 'French journeymen' in source 5), and one reason for his influence was his decision to bring out a cheap version of Part 2 of his Rights of Man, so that ordinary people could read it.

Source 4, taken with sources 2 and 5, also seems to disagree with the interpretation, as it says how fearful William Pitt was in 1792 – though it doesn't say anything about the years 1793–5. Certainly, Pitt's government was concerned enough to pass various acts which attempted to restrict the activities of radicals, such as the Proclamation against Wicked and Seditious Writings of 1792 (source 2), the suspension of Habeas Corpus in 1794 and the Seditious Meetings and Treason Acts of 1795 – as well as posters such as the one shown in source 5. In particular, there were worrying developments in Ireland, with the Society of United Irishmen, led by the republican Wolfe Tone – these hoped for a French invasion to help them achieve independence.

However, in Britain as a whole, support for the ideals of the French Revolution declined after 1793, following the executions of Louis XVI and Marie-Antoinette, the Terror, and the outbreak of war with France. Also, much protest during this period was linked to economic distress – such as when the wars disrupted the trade cycles, and the bad harvest of 1795 – rather than the ideals of the French Revolution. There were also plenty of anti-radical groups, such as the Association for the Protection of Property against Republicans and Levellers, which tried to limit the influence of pro-French groups by appealing to nationalism.

In conclusion, though some of the sources don't clearly disagree with the interpretation, overall they – and my own knowledge – suggest that the supporters of the French Revolution did offer a serious threat for a time, especially from 1792–3.

Examiner says:

A good introduction, which takes the sources as a whole and gives an overview. It shows an awareness of the need for a balanced evaluation of each source.

Examiner says:

This is a good mixture of using the content of the sources and dates of publication and adding some own knowledge.

Examiner says:

There is good cross-referencing of two sources – and some specific own knowledge.

Examiner says:

Examiners are looking for candidates to show skills in evaluating sources, e.g. comparing and contrasting content, nature, reliability and utility of sources, and using your own knowledge to challenge or support the news that they give.

Remember, also, to link your comments to the interpretation you are examining.

Exam Café
Relax, refresh, result!

European nationalism, 1815–1914: Germany and Italy

Relax and prepare

Hot tips
What I wish I had known at the start of the year…

Stuart

When I'm answering questions on sources, I try to remember to look at four things:

▷ Content (what the sources say)

▷ Provenance (nature, origin, purpose)

▷ Context (what was known/ happening at the time)

▷ Reliability/utility/typicality.

Hannah

Don't just re-write what a source says in the exam. Instead, pick out bits that help to answer the question one way or the other – and link each to your own knowledge: does what each source says fit the facts?

Bilal

I once lost marks because I made a general assumption about bias on the basis of affiliation/nationality, etc. Instead, check what they say against other sources and your own knowledge.

Refresh your memory

A revision checklist for German nationlism:

▷ **The constitution of 1871.** You should be aware of the emperor's (kaiser's) powers in the federal state. He was head of the executive and army, and had the right to declare war or martial law in an emergency. Ultimate power lay with the emperor.

▷ **The two houses of parliament.** There were two houses: the upper house (Bundesrat) consisted of representatives of the German states but, because Prussia was the biggest, it had the most representatives; the lower house (Reichstag) was elected by universal male suffrage every three years.

▷ **The reality of power.** In particular, the constitution was autocratic, with little power for the Reichstag. It had no control over the chancellor (who was appointed by and responsible to the emperor), and could not dismiss him. However, the Reichstag did have limited veto over legislation, and control over the federal budget.

▷ **Bismarck's relations with the Liberals.** At first, he relied on the Liberals for a majority in the Reichstag, as (in part) he needed their support against the Catholics. But this began to cool after 1874, and ended after disagreements over the Anti-Socialist Laws of 1878 and the free trade dispute in 1879. After 1879, he began to rely on the Conservative and Catholic Centre parties.

Common mistakes

Filiz

Avoid a 'shopping list' approach to sources, that's considering the sources in isolation, one after the other. Try to consider the sources in relation to the main issues they raise.

Get the result!

Examiner Tip:

Remember not to simply take the sources at face value. Use your knowledge of the period to interpret and evaluate them.

Exam question

Bismarck and the unification of Germany, 1848-71

Read the interpretation and sources 1–5.

Interpretation:
Bismarck's unification of Germany destroyed hopes of a liberal parliamentary regime.

(a) Explain how far sources 1–5 support this interpretation. You may, if you wish, amend the interpretation or suggest a different interpretation. If you do this, you must use the sources to support the changes you make. [35]

(b) Explain how these sources are both useful and raise problems and issues for a historian using them. [15]

Source 1

This historian sets out liberal criticisms of Bismarck's aims and methods:

'Bismarck's reputation was a mixed one. No one can deny his mastery of the political art; but many question his morality and his intentions. For liberal critics, he was and remains a great and evil man. They see him as an aggressor who used war as a conscious instrument of policy; as a cheat, who introduced democratic forms in order to preserve the undemocratic Prussian establishment; as a bully, who bludgeoned his opponents with the blunt instruments of state power.'

> N. Davies (1996) *A History of Europe*, in D.Murphy, *Do Brilliantly – A S European History, 1848 –1989 p. 24*.

Source 2

This writer states his fears about Prussian domination and the end of German liberty:

'No one can deny that intellectual and political freedom is better protected in a series of smaller states than in a powerful militaristic Prussian monarchy. The individual German states have given the people culture, morality and prosperity, together with civilizing and humanizing institutions, such as schools, universities and colleges of art and science. The variety of political, constitutional and administrative arrangements has safeguarded liberty in Germany. This will be destroyed under Prussian domination.'

> M. Mohr, 'For the attention of the South German States', September 1870.

Source 3

This historian stresses the undemocratic nature of the new constitution:

'Bismarck was determined that the offer of the Imperial crown should not, as in 1849, emanate from the people of Germany; it must come from the German princes. It was only after his fellow princes had joined with Ludwig [of Bavaria] in his proposal [to become German Emperor], that William consented to receive a deputation from the German Reichstag who made the same request on 19 December. Their President, Eduard Simson, had been the spokesman of the Frankfurt Assembly which had originally offered the Crown to Frederick William IV in 1849, but there the similarity with the epoch of liberal revolution ended. The entry of the south German states had been negotiated by Bismarck alone; the constitution of the new Empire was to be little different from that of the North German Confederation, an autocracy only slightly held in check by democratic forms, and the Imperial crown had been granted, as William II claimed in 1910, by "God's grace alone and not by parliaments, popular assemblies and popular decision".'

> A. Wood (1996) *Europe 1815–1960*, Longman, pp. 213 – 14.

Source 4

This historian questions the view that the Germany of 1871 was illiberal:

'Unification is often presented as a liberal surrender. That is one-sided and ignores those aspects of the process that liberals could welcome. After all, anything disliked by extreme conservatives, supporters of a divided Germany and Catholics was bound to have positive features for liberals. Unification created a self-governing, territorially defined national state with a constitution, parliament and chancellor. Liberals did not sacrifice 'liberal' values to the 'national' cause. The new Germany contained much that was central to liberal programmes: the rule of law, the legal accountability of ministers, freedom of movement, a liberal commercial code. These were not trivial matters to liberals, but a foundation on which they hoped to build a genuinely liberal state. They did not chose unity over freedom in 1871, but looked to extend freedom through unity in the coming years.'

> D. Blackbourn (1997) *Germany 1780–1918*.

Source 5

This historian argues that Bismarck tried to balance the needs of Prussia with the traditional rights of the other German states:

'In the North German Confederation, Bismarck sought to juggle various contending forces without making a mistake that would send everything crashing to the ground. By having 17 out of 43 seats on the Federal Council (Bundesrat), Prussia could prevent any change to the constitution. However, the historical tradition of the individual states' rights was too important to allow Prussia a dominant position in the new federal structure. Legal jurisdiction and matters of religion were left to the states. Federal laws required only a simple majority in the Federal Council, and this limited the Prussian veto to constitutional matters.'

> E. Dorn Brose (1997) *German History 1789–1871*

Stewart's answer: question (b)

These sources are useful, in that — between them — they give both sides of the argument, but they also present some problems. The majority (sources 1, 3, 4 and 5) are secondary sources, written by historians who have the benefit of hindsight. Presumably, they have no political purpose, as they seem to be academic History textbooks. However, there is only one primary source (source 2) — though it appears to be from a liberal, and seems typical of how some liberals felt in 1870–71; and most of the sources (with the exception of source 4) seem to take the same view — though source 5 does have a more balanced view.

Sources 1, 2 and 3 are useful, as the concerns expressed in source 2 are confirmed in sources 1 and 3, where source 1 states how liberal critics who feared Prussian domination saw Bismarck as introducing 'democratic forms to preserve the undemocratic Prussian establishment'; while source 3 stresses how Bismarck and the Kaiser were determined to avoid anything that hinted at the popular democracy connected to the hopes of liberals in the revolutions of 1848–9. In fact, the Constitution did consolidate the position that Prussia had enjoyed since the defeat of Austria in 1866; and Prussia, as the largest state, had 17 of the 43 seats in the Bundesrat — as stated in source 5. Although the Reichstag was elected every three years, Bismarck as Chancellor was not responsible to them, but to the Kaiser. Also, they could only vote on matters that Bismarck or the Bundesrat had initiated. This would support the liberal fears about the lack of real democracy mentioned in sources 1 and 2. However, sources 4 and 5 do point out that the Reichstag did have some control of the federal budget — but only as regards indirect taxes.

However, there are also some problems with the Sources — in particular, there is only one source (source 4) from a significantly different perspective. This is a lack, as there is debate about how far unification by 'Blood and Iron' led to Prussian domination as feared by the writer of source 2 — in particular, the ability to control constitutional change. However, there is some support of part of the content of source 4 in source 5.

Also, it would be good to have a source — preferably one not intended for publication — from Bismarck, giving his views and intentions about the Liberals and the constitution. An additional problem is that there are no sources from a contemporary Conservative, who might present a different view of 1871. Finally, there are no sources which refer to the splits amongst the liberals themselves — this took place in 1866, following the defeat of Austria, and led to the formation of the National Liberal party.

Examiner says:

This is a good introduction, taking the sources as a group and giving an overview, rather than treating them one by one.

Examiner says:

This is a good mixture of using the content of the sources, and adding some own knowledge to support or question what they argue.

Examiner says:

This is a good brief reference to relevant historical debate – and again includes some own knowledge to help judge them as the question demands.

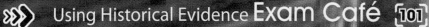

Bibliography

Chapter 1

Kekewich, L. and Rose, S. (1990) *The French Revolution*, Longman.

Warren, J. (1995) *The Wars of the Roses and the Yorkist Kings* (Access to History), Hodder & Stoughton.

Chapter 2

Armstrong, A. (2002) *The European Reformation*, Heinemann.

Philips, S. (2000) *Lenin and the Russian Revolution*, Heinemann.

Simpson, W. O. (1986) *Changing Horizons: Britain 1914–80*, Stanley Thornes.

Chapter 3

Clarke, C. (1962) *If the Nazis had Come*, Consul Books.

Duffy, E. (2001) Voices of *Morebath*, Yale University Press.

Fines, J. (1988) *Reading Historical Documents*, Basil Blackwell.

Fogel, R. (1964) *The Railroads and American Economic Growth*, John Hopkins Press.

Hartwell, R. M. (1961) 'The Rising Standard of Living in England, 1800–50', *Economic History Review*, 1961.

Hobsbawm, R. B. (1957) 'The British Standard of Living in England, 1800–50', *Economic History Review*.

Le Roy Ladurie, E. (1978) *Montaillou*, Penguin.

Mitchell, B. R. (1994) 'Statistics' in Caterall, P. (ed.) *Understanding Documents and Sources*, Heinemann History Briefings, Heinemann.

Thompson, E. P. (1967) 'Time and Work Discipline', *Past and Present*.

Chapter 4

Bettey, J. H. (1986) *Wessex from AD 1000*, Longman.

Cowie, L. W. and Wolfson, R. (1985) *Years of Nationalism*, Hodder & Stoughton.

Fletcher, A. (1983) *Tudor Rebellions*, Longman.

Richards, J. (2001) *Blood of the Vikings*, Hodder & Stoughton.

Viner, L. (2002) *Lost Villages*, Dovecote Press.

Wright, D. G. (1970) *Democracy and Reform 1815–1885*, Longman.

Useful reading

Black, J. and MacRaild, D. M. (2000) *Studying History*, 2nd edition, Macmillan.

Catterall, P. and Jones, H. (1994) *Understanding Documents and Sources*, Heinemann.

Marwick, A. (1970) *The Nature of History*, Macmillan.

Tosh, J. (1984) *The Pursuit of History*, Longman.

Magazines

BBC History magazine

History Review

History Today

20th Century History Review

Causal factors Causes of an event.

Causal mode (of explanation)
Historical method of enquiry used to explain events; based on arranging what happened into reasons, or causal factors, and showing how they brought about the event in question.

Conditional factors Factors that make an outcome possible and increasingly probable, or likely to happen.

Contextual knowledge Knowledge of the wider situation.

Contingent factors Factors that trigger the outcome to finally take place.

Counterfactual method Also known as the 'What if?' method; method of historical enquiry used to evaluate historical explanations by considering other possible outcomes and then explaining why they did not occur and the actual outcome that did.

Empathetic mode (of explanation)
Historical method of enquiry used to explain the nature, origins, development and appeal of the ideas that define attitudes and beliefs.

Historical dialectic Conflict of opposing forces, particularly linked to Marxist ideas.

Hypothesis An idea, or theory, based on existing evidence that claims to explain something.

Ideas The general attitudes and beliefs (sometimes called values, or value systems) that existed within a particular society or section of it.

Inference Things that are suggested or implied.

Intentional mode (of explanation)
Historical method of enquiry used to explain actions by considering the intentions and motives that lie behind them.

Provenance The origin and purpose of a source.

Regressive method Sometimes called 'backward progression'; method of historical enquiry based upon assumptions about how the present has been formed. It is most commonly associated with the historians of population (demographers).

Value systems Beliefs that existed within a particular society or section of it.

Index